# WAR OF WORDS

# WAR OF WORDS

## Language, Politics and 9/11

### SANDRA SILBERSTEIN

London and New York

First published 2002
by Routledge
11 New Fetter Lane, London EC4P 4EE

Simultaneously published in the USA and Canada
by Routledge
29 West 35th Street, New York, NY 10001

*Routledge is an imprint of the Taylor & Francis Group*

© 2002 Sandra Silberstein

Typeset in Baskerville by Bookcraft Ltd, Stroud, Gloucestershire
Printed and bound in Great Britain by MPG Books Ltd, Bodmin

*British Library, Cataloguing in Publication Data*
A catalogue record for this book is available from the British Library

*Library of Congress Cataloging in Publication Data*
A catalog record for this publication has been applied for

ISBN 0-415-29047-3

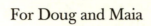

For Doug and Maia

# Contents

# Acknowledgments

I wish there had been no occasion for this book. When Routledge's Louisa Semlyen approached me in the summer of 2001 to write on George W. Bush, I told her nothing was happening. But I could have written a perfectly nice book on the political rhetoric of the early Bush administration. After the world changed on September 11, Louisa understood when I could think and write about nothing else. I am indebted and most grateful for Louisa's understanding and for the persistent and gentle prodding that assured the timely completion of this work.

Profound thanks are due to friends and colleagues who read drafts of the manuscript. They are unindictable for its shortcomings, but very much creditable for its strengths: Douglas N. Brown and Linda Stolfi did close reading far beyond the call of duty; Mark A. Clarke and Anis Bawarshi provided cogent feedback; Julie Scales spared me missteps and contributed her skills as a research sleuth.

As with any book, this one reflects the extraordinary patience of those around the author. Several communities have had to overlook my lapses and absences. I am deeply grateful for your understanding, and happy to be returning to everyday tasks.

Finally, words cannot capture my gratitude to my family. This is for you and the hope that by seeking to understand how our world comes to be, it can, by tiny increments, be made better.

The publishers would like to thank the following organizations for their help obtaining the following public service announcements:

The Arab-American Institute and the volunteer advertising agency *Brokaw*, for the PSA *Americans Stand United*.

Work, Inc. and the Ad Council, for the PSA *Indivisible*.

The National Crime Prevention Council and Saatchi and Saatchi, for the PSA *We all came over in different ships, but we're in the same boat now*.

The Ad Council, for the PSA *Racism Can Hide in the Strangest Places*.

Every effort has been made to obtain permission to reproduce copyright material. If any proper acknowledgment has not been made, or permission not received, we invite copyright holders to inform us of the oversight.

# Introduction

This book is about language, about the ways language is deployed in times of national crisis. In the aftermath of the events of September 11, through public rhetoric, an act of terror became a war; the Bush presidency was ratified; New York became America's city, with Rudy Giuliani as "mayor of the world." Patriotism became consumerism, dissent was discouraged, and Americans became students, newly schooled in strategic geography and Islam. Perhaps most importantly, public language (re)created a national identity.

I am an applied linguist by training and inclination. I study language as it is used in the world. And this is naturally the perspective I bring to the events of September 11. As that day began, planes flew into the World Trade Center and the Pentagon. Thereafter, words helped many things happen. That event was first termed an act of "terror" and then became an act of "war." "Acts of war" are typically reciprocated with other "acts of war"—but war against whom? To ask such questions is to take a critical linguistic lens to 9/11, to ask how language can be employed to render national policy common sense.

For me, these have not always been easy questions to ask, particularly in the context of tragedy. New York is my city of origin. I came of age on its streets, in its schools, in its libraries and parks. New York is a hometown, inspiring all the affections and allegiances accorded any birthplace around the globe. For me, it is important to honor the horror and loss of 9/11. Yet, New York is also a financial and cultural mecca, presumably attacked for that identity on September 11, 2001. One can examine the latter incarnation of the city without losing sight of the former; it is possible to mourn the losses of September 11 and still ask questions about it. This book explores the use of language in developing the public understanding of, and response to, the events that surrounded 9/11.

The linguistic trajectory from the World Trade Center and the Pentagon began with silence. No state announced responsibility for the events of September 11. But America was nonetheless assured that it had an "enemy,"—a "faceless enemy" that personified "evil." And against that evil, America came to wage a "new kind of war." The first step in that war, the first target, was Afghanistan. Because Afghanistan "harbored" the "faceless enemy," bombing of Afghanistan began on October 7, 2001.

This is the short version of the story. But much had to happen in what became known as "the homeland" before the bombing could be sanctioned at home. Through emblems of patriotism, the media endorsed, and indeed helped produce, "America's New War." Through public rhetoric, a rookie president, America's first appointed president, became popularly accepted as America's military commander in chief and America's chaplain. The nation was (re)created and united, with single purpose. The targets of the attacks were established—Western democracy, "our very way of life"—and one of the physical targets, New York, became America's city. Finally, dissent was discouraged. All of this occurred before a single bomb was dropped on Afghanistan, and all of this happened through words. How this process developed is the focus of this book.

Of course, political rhetoric is designed to be deployed in the service of public policy. As the War on Terrorism was formulated, familiar images and themes contributed to the consolidation of support for the Bush administration and for its prosecution of a war in Afghanistan. This is not to say that Americans are simply dupes of governmental and media propaganda. But increasingly the media produce an immersion in carefully crafted rhetoric and imagery. It is worth the effort to explore the interaction of the complex cultural strains that ultimately aided in building a consensus around war.

All cultures have within them multiple (often conflicting) discourses. In America we find strains of deep tolerance and multiculturalism; we also find racism and xenophobia. Public rhetoric can access these various strains, using them as raw material to (re)create a national perspective around notions that—because of their cultural resonance—are widely experienced as "common sense." In the case of the War on Terrorism, xenophobia could be used to create an intolerant "other" who supported attacks on our secular democracy. Once an "enemy" is positioned as "evil," fewer citizens are moved to inquire about "collateral damage," the precise situation for civilians "on the ground." To this day, amidst the enormous amount of discourse around the successes in Afghanistan, there is very little discussion about the human toll of the war.

The insights revealed by exploration of this rhetorical landscape are not always troubling; they can also be uplifting. Initially I had a cynical view of the deployment of the term *heroism*, as it was applied to anyone who had suffered on 9/11. But, ultimately I came to a different view—that the strain in American discourse that allowed for the broad use of that term came from a hearteningly altruistic ideology. Heroes became those who lost their lives selflessly helping others. There is much in the language of 9/11 to scrutinize and critique. And in the most difficult national moments, this is exactly what must be done. But there are also rhetorical moments that justify hope.

*War of Words* focuses largely on events in America immediately following the attacks of September 11, 2001. More specifically, it scrutinizes a range of language (visual, oral, written) produced in the wake of 9/11. It does not address the military events in Afghanistan and elsewhere. Rather, it explores the War of Words that made those events possible. Each chapter examines a different aspect of the War of Words through a different analytic lens.

*Chapter 1, "From Terror to War: The War on Terrorism":* In the weeks following 9/11, a terrorist attack comes to merit the full response of the U.S. military and the creation of an unprecedented coalition of allies. This chapter addresses the question: How did a response to terror become the War on Terrorism? The goal of this chapter is to detail how the particular road taken—the construction of a nation at war—is aided through the strategic deployment of language. This chapter examines presidential rhetoric.

*Chapter 2, "Becoming President"* explores another rhetorical turning point: the events of September 14, 2001. On that National Day of Prayer and Remembrance, the president addressed the nation at services in the National Cathedral, then visited "ground zero" in New York City. President Clinton's chief of staff, Leon Panetta, once observed, "Part of being president is being the nation's chaplain." This was the (rhetorical) role George W. Bush came to fulfill on that day.

*Chapter 3, "From News to Entertainment: Eyewitness Accounts":* In the wake of 9/11, the media was alive with survivors' tales—stories that captured horrifying events and the fortitude of those who survived them. Stories, by their nature, locate our very personal experiences within larger cultural norms and expectations. But for the televised narratives of September 11, their larger relevance was heavily constructed by reporters and the visual frames of the news media. Viewers were (re)made American through the televisual displays of the nation. This chapter examines the role of television in creating accounts of September 11 and in constructing post-9/11 identities. The chapter focuses on approaches to studying narrative as it moves from "real time" story-telling to the highly manufactured tales that appeared on news magazines and on a prime-time series. This discussion is the most linguistic in the book.

*Chapter 4, "New York Becomes America(n)":* Perhaps for the first time since 1790—when it ceased being the federal capital—New York became archetypically American on 9/11. On that day, New York became America. With the exception of scant coverage from the Pentagon (a military target), news coverage emanated from New York. The Twin Towers, a symbol of New York, became the symbol of "The Attack on America." The "innocent civilians" attacked as presumptive Americans were New Yorkers. This chapter explores the rhetorical construction of New York as an American city and Rudy Giuliani as America's mayor.

*Chapter 5, "Selling America":* Two kinds of campaigns "sold America" post-September 11. One was a manifestation of nation building as it sold America on itself. "I am an American," was probably one of the most successful public service announcements in the history of the republic. The second campaign sold America on consumerism. Both promotions turned on patriotism. One built loyalty to values of tolerance and diversity. The other conflated patriotism and consumerism in a dance of political/economic codependence, resisted (at least initially) by many. The trajectory of these promotional campaigns—from tolerance to spending—is the focus of this chapter.

*Chapter 6, "'The New McCarthyism'":* Along with increased patriotism, post-9/11 saw attacks on those who questioned U.S. policy. A provoking volley was fired by the conservative American Council of Trustees and Alumni (ACTA), founded by Lynne Cheney, wife of the Vice President. In November, ACTA published a report listing more than 100 examples of what it claimed was a "blame America first" attitude on America's campuses. While ACTA tarred campuses as a "weak link," some on campus found the ACTA report truly sinister. "The New McCarthyism" examines the ACTA campaign and reactions to it. Part of the rhetorical analysis centers on logical fallacies.

*Chapter 7, "Schooling America: Lessons on Islam and Geography":* After the attack on America, made in the name of Islam, the media sought to inform an audience admittedly unacquainted with both the religion and a region that is home to more than a billion Muslims. This was not a benign travelogue of cultural and historical highpoints. Rather, instruction focused on the military, political, and economic self-interest of the United States. "Schooling America" focuses on these pedagogical moments.

## TRANSCRIPTION CONVENTIONS

A word on transcription is in order. Linguists have their own arcane transcription conventions, which defy traditional punctuation. To make this text accessible to nonlinguists, I elected to use traditional punctuation when transcribing speech. I did, however, use a few linguistic conventions. If one speaker overlapped the talk of another, I used a square bracket "[" to indicate where that overlap began. I chose to maintain speakers' actual false starts, often indicating these with a hyphen: "word- ." Also maintained are the fillers speakers used in natural conversation, so readers will find *ah*s and *um*s sprinkled throughout. Additionally worth noting is that, for clarity's sake, some words in example texts are bolded to indicate the basis of claims and analyses. Finally, I took a decision to avoid the use of *sic* throughout the text. In the rush of the moment, many people misspeak, and it seemed uncalled for to indicate each time such an error occurred. I also found the punctuation on the White House and other Web sites somewhat idiosyncratic, but I judged it inappropriate to pepper transcripts of presidential speeches, for example, with *sic*. This book is about the way language is actually used, and I have tried to capture that sense of things in the texts that appear throughout.

# 1

# From Terror to War
## The War on Terrorism

Presidential power is the power to persuade.
                                    Political scientist Richard Neustadt[1]

At 8:45 a.m. EDT on the morning of September 11, 2001, an American Airlines jet flew into the north tower of the World Trade Center. With the collision of a second plane, into the south tower, it became clear that the media was not covering an accident. This was confirmed within the hour as an American Airlines plane flew into the Pentagon and another hijacked flight crashed south of Pittsburgh. CNN banners screamed "Breaking News" above "America Under Attack." And for several days thereafter, CNN announced the "Attack on America." But the "attack" quickly became an act of war, this generation's "Pearl Harbor." It is not the intent of this chapter or this book to speak to the validity of this analysis. (My cousins, academic historians living in lower Manhattan, found it impossible not to feel themselves in a war—witnessing war crimes against innocent civilians.) Nonetheless, given that other rhetorical and political postures were available, the goal in this discussion is to detail how the particular road taken—the construction of a nation at war—is aided through the strategic deployment of language.

The perspective I will be taking is that language has consequences—that through the use of language, we create and recreate particular worlds of understanding. For this reason, I will sometimes be using the convention of parentheses when I talk about (re)creating, for example, a unified nation.

Examining presidential rhetoric in the wake of September 11, we see a terrorist attack that comes to merit the full response of the U.S. military and the creation of an unprecedented coalition of allies. This chapter addresses the question, how did a response to terror become the War on Terrorism?

First, a few words on terrorism. Unfortunately for those of us living in this electronic age, terrorism is an act made for television. Terrorism specialist Walter Laqueur notes:

> The success of a terrorist operation depends almost entirely on the amount of publicity it receives. This is one of the main reasons for the shift from rural guerrilla to urban terror in the 1960s; for in the cities the terrorist could always count on the presence of journalists and TV cameras and consequently a large audience.[2]

Terrorism feeds on the news media in a system of mutual survival. Former diplomat David Long notes: "The media's mission to cover the news and the terrorist's ability to 'create' news have led to a symbiotic relationship between the two, one in which the media not only convey the news, but help the terrorist create it." Terrorist violence succeeds in the form of "carefully planned theatrical events."[3]

Terrorist attacks are a particular challenge to a government that must create the impression that it is able to contain violence and protect its citizens. It must find a balance between appearing ineffectual and infringing on civil liberties.[4] And it needs to ensure that terrorists don't dominate the news. This creates a presidency dependent on media exposure for its own power to persuade.

In effect, the media age has transformed the very office of the U.S. presidency. Roderick Hart[5] characterizes its modern role: "the president is first and foremost a talker." Prior to the twentieth century, he reports, "presidents rarely spoke at all." But all that was to change. Between 1945 and 1975, public speeches by U.S. presidents increased almost 500%. And that figure has continued to increase.[6] Hart again: "presidential speech and action increasingly reflect the opinion that speaking *is* governing." The power of the presidency rests in its ability to persuade.

And that power and persuasion rests in access to the media and the ability to shape reporting. Even though terrorists create televised events, communications specialist Steven Livingston argues that the ability to shape reporting remains the province of the government:

> The power to shape perceptions of violent events and their principal actors (both perpetrators and victims) usually rests not with the terrorists but with government officials. Who the terrorists are in the first place is a question largely determined by these officials. Those who have routine access to the mass media, those to whom reporters turn when the dust settles and the shooting stops, have the ability to shape coverage and perceptions.[7]

Such was the office and the task on 9/11 when George W. Bush addressed the nation. Presidential speeches draw news coverage, and Bush would speak to the nation three times that first day, including a prime-time address. These speeches can be found in the Appendix to this chapter. In addition, there would be four press briefings by the White House and a statement by the press secretary. And, of course, statements by current and former government officials would fill the airwaves.

Bush's first remarks came a scant forty-five minutes after the first plane hit; he spoke for only a minute from Emma Booker Elementary School in Sarasota, Florida.[8] In a brief statement, Bush described the events with noteworthy precision: "Two airplanes have crashed into the World Trade Center." He also characterized the situation: "a difficult moment for America," "an apparent terrorist attack," and "a national tragedy." America was not yet at war.

In examining the next two sentences, we'll take a close look at the language used, particularly the grammatical choices. These remarks also participate in the rhetorical (re)construction of the presidential Bush. He is in control—grammatically marked as an active agent. In the following quote, note the use of the personal pronoun, *I*, and the use of the active voice as Bush marshals the full resources of the state:

> I have spoken to the Vice President, to the Governor of New York, to the Director of the FBI, and have ordered that the full resources of the federal government go to help the victims and their families,

and to conduct a full-scale investigation to hunt down and to find those folks who committed this act.

This phrasing stands in sharp contrast to comments made by Attorney General John Ashcroft later in the day.[9] His statements are grammatically "passive": "Crime scenes **have been** established by the federal authorities." And some statements have no agent: "The full resources of the Department of Justice ... **are being deployed** to investigate these crimes and to assist survivors and victim families." In the president's remarks, he personally had done everything possible to help and protect the citizens.

The president is firm, "Terrorism against our nation will not stand." In pledging to find "**those folks** who committed this act" he has been both presidential and folksy. As one scholar has observed, "The presidency is still a damned informal monarchy."[10]

Grammatically, the president creates a united nation, under God. "**We've** had a **national** tragedy," he reports. In examining the use of pronouns here, we have what linguist John Wilson calls a "pronominal window into the thinking and attitudes"[11] of a political leader. Oftentimes the referent for the pronouns *we* and *you* is ambiguous (as "we'll" recall from the exhortations of "our" high school teachers to avoid their use!). There is certainly ambiguity in the phrasing by Health and Human Services Secretary Thompson later in the day: "It is now **our** mission to begin the healing from this tragedy." In contrast, Bush's "we" is the nation (re)created and united through his remarks: "Terrorism against **our nation** will not stand." Having constructed the listeners as a nation, Bush ends with a nation under God: "And now if you would join me in a moment of silence. May God bless the victims, their families, and America. Thank you very much."

With the attack on the Pentagon and the downing of Flight 93—which may have been heading for the White House—those charged with presidential security faced a dilemma. On the one hand, the president had to be kept in secure locations. On the other hand, he needed to be rhetorically visible. The president spoke again at 1:04 p.m. from Barksdale Air Force Base in Louisiana.[12] His first task is reassurance; he begins: "I want to reassure the American people that the full resources of the federal government are working to assist local authorities to save lives and to help the victims of these attacks." Once again, notwithstanding the president's absence from the capital, he is able to confirm that he has marshaled the full resources of the state. He is also able to reassure those for whom talking is governing: "I've been in regular contact with the Vice President, the Secretary of Defense, the national security team and my Cabinet." And that talk has worked in the service of the people's government: "we have taken the necessary security precautions to continue the functions of **your** government" and in the service of their safety: "We have taken all appropriate security precautions to protect the American people."

For those listening carefully for clues to planned military actions, there are several key phrases. The first does not seem to put the United States on a war footing: "Make no mistake: The United States will hunt down and punish those responsible for these cowardly acts." Hunting down and punishing could indicate covert actions, leading to, for example, assassination or bringing perpetrators to justice under U.S. or international law. It could also mean formal military action. The next clue comes quickly: "We have been in touch with the leaders of Congress and with world leaders to assure them that we will do whatever is necessary to protect America and Americans." This phrasing is more ominous. When the president speaks, he governs. And the courtesies of warning allies in advance of attacks may begin to be in place.

The president is firm. Twice he says, "make no mistake." The second time can also be read in a military context, as he addresses the rhetorically unified nation: "The resolve of **our** great nation is being tested. But make no mistake: We will show the world that we will pass this test."

The Barksdale statement is similar to the first: It places the president in charge, bringing to the service of the people the resources of the state. But it expands on the single statement made earlier, "Terrorism against our nation will not stand." In the second brief statement, assurances of resolve are accompanied by assurances of action: "we will do whatever is necessary."

The president closes as he had previously, on a religious note. Just before indicating that the nation would pass the test, he thanks "the folks" who were mounting the rescue efforts, and offers a prayer for victims and families. Bush ends with "God bless."

By the evening, we had "the war on terrorism," announced in the course of a five-minute, prime-time address to the nation.[13] The president begins by characterizing the attacks. They are no longer "two airplanes [crashing] into the World Trade Center." Nor are they simply "traged[ies]." Rather, they are attacks on "our way of life."

> Good evening. Today, our fellow citizens, our way of life, our very freedom came under attack in a series of deliberate and deadly terrorist acts. The victims were in airplanes, or in their offices; secretaries, businessmen and women, military and federal workers; moms and dads, friends and neighbors. Thousands of lives were suddenly ended by evil, despicable acts of terror.

Within a few short lines, much has been accomplished rhetorically. A "fellow citizenry" has been invoked–united within its symbolic territory of a "way of life" and its "freedoms." To invoke those symbols is to invoke precepts for which, I daresay, most Americans would give their/ our lives. To understand how these concepts can be deployed rhetorically, it's necessary to say a few words about both nation and symbols.

Anthropologist Benedict Anderson[14] defines the nation as "an imagined political community." It is imagined, he tells us, "because the members of even the smallest nation will never know most of their fellow-members, meet them or even hear of them, yet in the minds of each lives the image of their communion." Moreover, national boundaries tend to be recent, elastic, and accidental. As a philosophical entity, he argues, nation-states are rather impoverished. Nonetheless, today, all individuals on the planet are born into nations.

Literary scholar Lauren Berlant[15] (1991) explores American nation building. She argues that Americans are "inextricably bound together by America. ... because we inhabit the political space of the nation." This space is not merely legal, geographical, genetic, linguistic, or experiential, but "some tangled cluster of all of these." She calls this political space the "national symbolic"–a place that brings together all the symbols that evoke America. Following Berlant, the rhetorical terrain of September 11 can be thought of as a national symbolic site. Berlant argues that through our linguistic practices we continually (re)create the nation. And one of the goals of the national symbolic is to produce a fantasy of national integration. In fact, this integration is the utopian promise of the nation. Through national identity, the individual is liberated from solely local affiliations and promised an almost limitless collective identity. But Berlant notes, "people are not naturally 'the people' in their local affiliations."[16] Nations must be (re)made. Media coverage of the Olympics, for example, promises my young daughter collective identity and renews the nation, even (or especially?) when our athletes are "under attack."

In President Bush's prime-time speech, those eligible, are (re)made Americans—under attack, in airplanes and offices; moms and dads. America's symbolic terrain is the site from which this speech is delivered:

> A great people has been moved to defend a great nation. Terrorist attacks can shake the foundations of our biggest buildings, but they cannot touch the foundation of America. These acts shattered steel, but they cannot dent the steel of American resolve.
>
> America was targeted for attack because we're the brightest beacon for freedom and opportunity in the world. And no one will keep that light from shining.
>
> Today our nation saw evil, the very worst of human nature. And we responded with the best of America—with the daring of our rescue workers, with the caring for strangers and neighbors who came to give blood and help in any way they could.
>
> This is a day when all Americans from every walk of life unite in our resolve for justice and peace. America has stood down enemies before, and we will do so this time. None of us will ever forget this day. Yet, we go forward to defend freedom and all that is good and just in our world.

One aspect of this nation-building rhetoric is "convergence by divergence."[17] Americans are brought together through their contrast with a shared enemy. Evil and the worst in human nature are met by the best in America—daring and caring. "Despicable acts" and "mass murder" are contrasted with "the brightest beacon of freedom," justice, and peace. These contrasts will be maintained throughout the rhetorical war. And they will be used by allied heads of state who need to rally their citizens. Britain's Prime Minister Tony Blair states on September 11, "The people who perpetrate this have no regard whatever for the sanctity or value of human life, and we the democracies of the world, must come together. ...."[18] He echoes these remarks on September 12:

> [T]he world now knows the full evil and capability of international terrorism which menaces the whole of the democratic world. The terrorists responsible have no sense of humanity, of mercy, or of justice.
>
> To commit acts of this nature requires a fanaticism and wickedness that is beyond our normal contemplation.[19]

Presidential rhetoric has been said to have two styles.[20] The first is *motivational*, which is high on optimism, low on specific programs. The second is termed *pedagogical*, which is high on realism and certainty, and symbolism framed in human terms. In some sense, presidents must communicate both tendencies. "The president ... is the nation's first chauvinist as well as its most dependable teacher."[21] But individual presidents tend toward one style or the other. Ironically, George W. Bush, long the butt of jokes for his unschooled demeanor, displays a highly pedagogical style—one that becomes increasingly pedagogical in the days to come. In this 9/11 address, the symbols of America invoked in Bush's speech are framed very much within human terms, and within descriptions of unflagging realism and certainty. We see this clearly when Bush describes realistically the context, then adds with certainty that the nation will prevail:

> The pictures of airplanes flying into buildings, fires burning, huge structures collapsing, have filled us with disbelief, terrible sadness, and a quiet, unyielding anger. These acts of mass murder were intended to frighten our nation into chaos and retreat. But they have failed; our country is strong.

The president speaks with certainty throughout the speech when he asserts:

> Our military is powerful, and it's prepared.
>
> The functions of our government continue without interruption.

Our financial institutions remain strong.

America has stood down enemies before, and we will do so this time.

With confident realism Bush continues the presidential countenance built throughout the day. He announces steps he has taken as the nation's chief executive:

Immediately following the first attack, I implemented our government's emergency response plans.

I've directed the full resources of our intelligence and law enforcement communities to find those responsible and to bring them to justice.

And there are new ways in which Bush signals presidential prerogatives. Notice the following two statements:

I appreciate so very much the members of Congress who have joined me in strongly condemning these attacks.

And on behalf of the American people, I thank the many world leaders who have called to offer their condolences and assistance.

In the first statement, condemnations are construed not as independent statements, but as declarations that join the president. In the second, Bush speaks "on behalf of the American people." In both cases, the language foregrounds presidential prerogatives–the ability to set the agenda and to speak for the nation. Not foregrounded, but rather announced as already given information, is the confirmation of building support: both the Congress and many world leaders are on board.

Announcing the building coalition allows the first reference to war:

America and our friends and allies join with all those who want peace and security in the world, and we stand together to win the **war against terrorism**.

In support of that war, the president asks once again that "God bless America."

In his first formal speech of the day, President Bush has set into motion the themes that will accompany U.S. policy and actions for the foreseeable future: Evil, Terror, and the War on Terrorism.

Rhetorically, the president is very much in step with the public. As we will see in Chapter 3, "From News to Entertainment: Eyewitness Accounts," the public was quick to label September 11 an act of terrorism. Immediately after the attacks, person-on-the-street Colleen refers to the hijackers as "zealot terrorist pigs." And she goes further, installing Bush as the commander in chief, who will take whatever actions are necessary: "Whatever we have to do to eradicate the country or the world of this- of this vermin, I just hope Bush will do whatever is necessary to get rid of them."

Colleen's remarks reflect the realities of modern U.S. military action. Rhetoricians Campbell and Jamieson explain:

> The rhetorical model in the Constitution is that of a president going to Congress to request authorization for acting as commander in chief; the model that has developed through time is that of a president assuming that role and asking for congressional ratification.[22]

This situation is recognized by the 1973 War Powers Act, which allows the president to enter United States Armed Forces into combat in the absence of a formal declaration of war. Its insistence that troops be recalled within a specified period of time has never been tested.

Rhetorically, Campbell and Jamieson note that, over time, the constitutional rhetoric of cooperation between the president and Congress has been replaced by one of justification. They argue that presidential war rhetoric throughout U.S. history displays five characteristics:

> (1) every element in it proclaims that the momentous decision to resort to force is deliberate, the product of thoughtful consideration; (2) forceful intervention is justified through a chronicle or narrative from which argumentative claims are drawn; (3) the audience is exhorted to unanimity of purpose and total commitment; (4) the rhetoric not only justifies the use of force but also

seeks to legitimate presidential assumption of the extraordinary powers of the commander in chief; and as a function of these other characteristics; (5) strategic misrepresentations play an unusually significant role in its appeals.[23]

Many of these features will be familiar from our discussion thus far. War rhetoric, after all, dominated White House communication after September 11. Maintaining some of the conventions of war, the president addressed a joint session of Congress and the American people on September 20.[24] (This speech can be found in the Appendix to this chapter.) His persuasive task was made easier in the context of a joint congressional resolution on September 12, which had already committed money to the War on Terrorism and supported the president, "in close consultation with the Congress, to bring to justice and punish the perpetrators of these attacks as well as their sponsors."

The president's September 20 address was highly pedagogical. He addresses Campbell and Jamieson's first imperative—to demonstrate thoughtful deliberation—through the use of a series of questions, which are answered carefully and at length. We'll look only at the questions here:

Americans have many questions tonight. Americans are asking: Who attacked our country?

Americans are asking, why do they hate us?

Americans are asking: How will we fight and win this war?

Americans are asking: What is expected of us?

Again, in keeping with Campbell and Jamieson, the War on Terrorism is justified by a chronicle:

On September 11th, enemies of freedom committed an act of war against our country. Americans have known wars—but for the past 136 years, they have been wars on foreign soil, except for one Sunday in 1941. Americans have known the casualties of war—but not at the center of a great city on a peaceful morning. Americans have known surprise attacks—but never before on thousands of civilians. All of this, was brought upon us in a single day—and night fell on a different world, a world where freedom itself is under attack.

The audience is exhorted to unity of purpose and commitment. The litany that asks for commitment begins with a presidential "I ask you":

> I ask you to uphold the values of America, and remember why so many have come here.
>
> I ask you to continue to support the victims of this tragedy with your contributions.
>
> I ask for your patience, with the delays and inconveniences that may accompany tighter security; and for your patience in what will be a long struggle.
>
> I ask for your continued participation and confidence in the American economy.
>
> And finally, please continue praying.

Americans are not being asked to give their lives here, but this is suggested at another point, as we'll see below. The litany that seeks unanimity of purpose begins with "we will come together":

> We will come together to improve air safety.
>
> We will come together to give law enforcement the additional tools it needs to track down terror here at home.
>
> We will come together to take active steps that strengthen America's economy, and to put our people back to work.

The unity that is sought, however, is also global:

> This is not, however, just America's fight. And what is at stake is not just America's freedom. This is the world's fight. This is civilization's fight. This is the fight of all who believe in progress and pluralism, tolerance and freedom.
>
> We ask every nation to join us. ...

The civilized world is rallying to America's side. ...

Bush is on strong rhetorical ground here. Earlier in the day, Tony Blair had announced, "This is not a battle between the United States of America and terrorism, but between the free and democratic world and terrorism. We, therefore, here in Britain stand shoulder to shoulder with our American friends." On September 12, he confirms this unity after conversations with "several world leaders":

> We all agreed that this attack is an attack not only on America but on the world, which demands our complete and united condemnation, our determination to bring those responsible to justice and our support for the American people at this time of trial.

Having sought unity and commitment, Bush's speech also acknowledges his role as commander in chief:

> We will direct every resource at our command—every means of diplomacy, every tool of intelligence, every instrument of law enforcement, every financial influence, and every necessary weapon of war—to the disruption and to the defeat of the global terror network.

In keeping with a pedagogical style, the speech is filled with realism and certainty. Realistically, it describes a new kind of war, a war that can lead to loss of life:

> This war will not be like the war against Iraq a decade ago, with a decisive liberation of territory and a swift conclusion. It will not look like the air war above Kosovo two years ago, where no ground troops were used and not a single American was lost in combat.

> Our response involves far more than instant retaliation and isolated strikes. Americans should not expect one battle, but a lengthy campaign, unlike any other we have ever seen. It may include dramatic strikes, visible on TV, and covert operations, secret even in success.

Certainty rests in the result of the war, not in its trajectory: While "the course of this conflict is not known ... its outcome is certain."

As in previous speeches, strong contrasting lines are drawn:

Every nation, in every region, now has a decision to make. Either you are with us, or you are with the terrorists.

Freedom and fear, justice and cruelty, have always been at war, and we know that God is not neutral between them.

In many ways this address, announcing a new kind of war, asking commitment of the public, is very much like the standard war rhetoric documented since the beginning of the republic. Hindsight will tell us the extent to which the speech conforms to Campbell and Jamieson's fifth characteristic: strategic misrepresentation, a feature that would likely be more prominent in the absence of a clear attack. Their use of the term *misrepresentation* is an attempt to capture the special context of war rhetoric. In assuming the role of a wartime commander in chief, a president is exercising extraordinary powers, powers that are comfortably granted in a democracy only in the context of a very strong consensus. Speeches designed to minimize dissent and build unity will necessarily report selectively and slant at least through emphasis. The potential for this selectivity is created by the fact that only the president has access to the information that will determine whether military action will be taken.

Campbell and Jamieson stress that misrepresentation comes often in the form of omissions. In this address, the sole grievance acknowledged for Al Qaeda, the sole response given to the question "why do they hate us?" is that "they hate our freedoms." Arguably the resentments that fuel Al Qaeda recruitment go beyond that, and more thoughtful commentary in the weeks to come would explore the making of terrorists. But that was not the rhetorical task at hand. (And we will see in Chapter 6, "'The New McCarthyism,'" that some who questioned these strategic misrepresentations were excoriated in print.)

Along with the description of Al Qaeda's grievances, the characterization of Al Qaeda itself is questionable: "its goal is … imposing its radical beliefs on people everywhere." This is, at best, a simplification.

Finally, it's important to note that the imminent bombing of Afghanistan could only be justified by conflating the Taliban with Al Qaeda ("In Afghanistan, we see Al Qaeda's vision for the world"), arguably a misrepresentation, even if in the minds of many it would not be considered a very great one. Had there been more civilian casualties in the U.S. air strikes, this conflation would have loomed larger in the days and weeks that followed. But initially, few civilian casualties were reported, and few Americans would have grieved over the Taliban as "collateral damage."

There are other potential omissions. President Bush's rhetoric does not detail why war becomes the inevitable response to terrorism. Nor is there a discussion of the other consequences resulting from war, for example, the expansion of American military power and presence worldwide.

The final rhetorical moment in the construction of the War on Terrorism came on October 7, when the president addressed the nation from the White House Treaty Room to announce the bombing of Afghanistan.[25] He began, "On my orders, the United States military has begun strikes against Al Qaeda terrorist training camps and military installations of the Taliban regime in Afghanistan." For the first time in more than half a century, the U.S. was responding to an attack on its territory. Comparing President Bush's speeches with Roosevelt's famous "Day of Infamy" address[26] and his fireside chat[27] the next day (both in the Appendix to this chapter), it becomes clear that nations are not brought rhetorically to war in a single speech. Rather, the persuasive efforts of American presidents are ongoing, suggesting that studies of a single Declaration of War are at best incomplete. What is also clear is that while the War on Terrorism may be an untraveled road, its rhetorical route is well-trodden.

We'll end this chapter by comparing the presidential rhetoric of Pearl Harbor with that of September 11. Through rhetorical conventions, presidents assume extraordinary powers as the commander in chief, dissent is minimized, enemies are vilified, and lives are lost in the defense of a nation once again united under God. So ritualized has been the invocation of prayer and divinity, this feature could well be added as a sixth characteristic of the American rhetoric of war. The role of prayer will be examined in Chapter 2, "Becoming President."

12/8/41: Yesterday, December 7, 1941, a date that will live in infamy, the United States of America was suddenly and deliberately attacked.

9/11/01: Today, our fellow citizens, our very freedom came under attack in a series of deliberate and deadly terrorist acts.

12/9/41: Many American soldiers and sailors have been killed by enemy action. American ships have been sunk; American airplanes have been destroyed.

9/11/01: The victims were in airplanes, or in their offices; secretaries, businessmen and women, military and federal workers; moms and dad, friends and neighbors.

12/9/41: Powerful and resourceful gangsters have banded together to make war upon the whole human race.

9/20/01: Al Qaeda is to terror what the mafia is to crime. But its goal is not making money; its goal is remaking the world—and imposing its radical beliefs on people everywhere.

9/9/41: There is no such thing as security for any nation—or any individual—in a world ruled by the principles of gangsterism.

10/7/01: There can be no peace in a world of sudden terror.

9/9/41: We are now in the midst of a war, not for conquest, not for vengeance, but for a world in which this nation, and all that this nation represents, will be safe for our children.

9/20/01: The advance of human freedom—the great achievement of our time, and the great hope of every time—now depends on us. Our nation—this generation—will lift a dark threat of violence from our people and our future.

12/7/41: As Commander in Chief of the Army and Navy I have directed that all measures be taken for our defense.

9/20/01: We will direct every resource at our command—every means of diplomacy, every tool of intelligence, every instrument of law enforcement, every financial influence, and every necessary weapon of war—to the disruption and to the defeat of the global terror network.

12/8/41: It will not be a long war, it will be a hard war.

9/20/01: Americans should not expect one battle, but a lengthy campaign, unlike any other we have ever seen.

12/9/41: We will know that the vast majority of the members of the human race are on our side. Many of them are fighting with us.

9/20/01: The civilized world is rallying to America's side.

12/8/41: With confidence in our armed forces with the unbounded determination of our people we will gain the inevitable triumph so help us God.

10/7/01: We will not waver; we will not tire; we will not falter; and we will not fail. Peace and freedom will prevail. May God continue to bless America.

# Appendix

## REMARKS BY THE PRESIDENT AFTER TWO PLANES CRASH INTO WORLD TRADE CENTER, EMMA BOOKER ELEMENTARY SCHOOL, SARASOTA, FLORIDA

September 11, 2001, 9:30 a.m. EDT

THE PRESIDENT  Ladies and gentlemen, this is a difficult moment for America. I, unfortunately, will be going back to Washington after my remarks. Secretary Rod Paige and the Lt. Governor will take the podium and discuss education. I do want to thank the folks here at Booker Elementary School for their hospitality.

Today we've had a national tragedy. Two airplanes have crashed into the World Trade Center in an apparent terrorist attack on our country. I have spoken to the Vice President, to the Governor of New York, to the Director of the FBI, and have ordered that the full resources of the federal government go to help the victims and their families, and to conduct a full-scale investigation to hunt down and to find those folks who committed this act.

Terrorism against our nation will not stand.

And now if you would join me in a moment of silence. May God bless the victims, their families, and America. Thank you very much.

http://www.whitehouse.gov/news/releases/2001/09/20010911.html

## REMARKS BY THE PRESIDENT UPON ARRIVAL AT BARKSDALE AIR FORCE BASE, LOUISIANA

September 11, 2001

THE PRESIDENT  I want to reassure the American people that the full resources of the federal government are working to assist local authorities to save lives and to help the victims of these attacks. Make no mistake: The United States will hunt down and punish those responsible for these cowardly acts.

I've been in regular contact with the Vice President, the Secretary of Defense, the national security team and my Cabinet. We have taken all appropriate security precautions to protect the American people. Our military at home and around the world is on high alert status, and we have taken the necessary security precautions to continue the functions of your government.

We have been in touch with the leaders of Congress and with world leaders to assure them that we will do whatever is necessary to protect America and Americans.

I ask the American people to join me in saying a thanks for all the folks who have been fighting hard to rescue our fellow citizens and to join me in saying a prayer for the victims and their families.

The resolve of our great nation is being tested. But make no mistake: We will show the world that we will pass this test. God bless.

http://www.whitehouse.gov/news/releases/2001/09/20010911-1.html

## STATEMENT BY THE PRESIDENT IN HIS ADDRESS TO THE NATION

September 11, 2001, 8:30 p.m. EDT

THE PRESIDENT  Good evening. Today, our fellow citizens, our way of life, our very freedom came under attack in a series of deliberate and deadly terrorist acts. The victims were in airplanes, or in their offices; secretaries, businessmen and women, military and federal workers; moms and dads, friends and neighbors. Thousands of lives were suddenly ended by evil, despicable acts of terror.

The pictures of airplanes flying into buildings, fires burning, huge structures collapsing, have filled us with disbelief, terrible sadness, and a quiet, unyielding anger. These acts of mass murder were intended to frighten our nation into chaos and retreat. But they have failed; our country is strong.

A great people has been moved to defend a great nation. Terrorist attacks can shake the foundations of our biggest buildings, but they cannot touch the foundation of America. These acts shattered steel, but they cannot dent the steel of American resolve.

America was targeted for attack because we're the brightest beacon for freedom and opportunity in the world. And no one will keep that light from shining.

Today, our nation saw evil, the very worst of human nature. And we responded with the best of America—with the daring of our rescue workers, with the caring for strangers and neighbors who came to give blood and help in any way they could.

Immediately following the first attack, I implemented our government's emergency response plans. Our military is powerful, and it's prepared. Our emergency teams are working in New York City and Washington, D.C. to help with local rescue efforts.

Our first priority is to get help to those who have been injured, and to take every precaution to protect our citizens at home and around the world from further attacks.

The functions of our government continue without interruption. Federal agencies in Washington which had to be evacuated today are reopening for essential personnel tonight, and will be open for business tomorrow. Our financial institutions remain strong, and the American economy will be open for business, as well.

The search is underway for those who are behind these evil acts. I've directed the full resources of our intelligence and law enforcement communities to find those responsible and to bring them to justice. We will make no distinction between the terrorists who committed these acts and those who harbor them.

I appreciate so very much the members of Congress who have joined me in strongly condemning these attacks. And on behalf of the American people, I thank the many world leaders who have called to offer their condolences and assistance.

America and our friends and allies join with all those who want peace and security in the world, and we stand together to win the war against terrorism. Tonight, I ask for your prayers for all those who grieve, for the children whose worlds have been shattered, for all whose sense of safety and security has been threatened. And I pray they will be comforted by a power greater than any of us, spoken through the ages in Psalm 23: "Even though I walk through the valley of the shadow of death, I fear no evil, for You are with me."

This is a day when all Americans from every walk of life unite in our resolve for justice and peace. America has stood down enemies before, and we will do so this time. None of us will ever forget this day. Yet, we go forward to defend freedom and all that is good and just in our world.

Thank you. Good night, and God bless America.

http://www.whitehouse.gov/news/releases/2001/09/20010911-16.html

## ADDRESS TO A JOINT SESSION OF CONGRESS AND THE AMERICAN PEOPLE, UNITED STATES CAPITOL, WASHINGTON, D.C.

September 20, 2001, 9:00 p.m. EDT

**THE PRESIDENT** Mr. Speaker, Mr. President Pro Tempore, members of Congress, and fellow Americans:

In the normal course of events, Presidents come to this chamber to report on the state of the Union. Tonight, no such report is needed. It has already been delivered by the American people.

We have seen it in the courage of passengers, who rushed terrorists to save others on the ground—passengers like an exceptional man named Todd Beamer. And would you please help me to welcome his wife, Lisa Beamer, here tonight. (Applause.)

We have seen the state of our Union in the endurance of rescuers, working past exhaustion. We have seen the unfurling of flags, the lighting of candles, the giving of blood, the saying of prayers—in English, Hebrew, and Arabic. We have seen the decency of a loving and giving people who have made the grief of strangers their own.

My fellow citizens, for the last nine days, the entire world has seen for itself the state of our Union—and it is strong. (Applause.)

Tonight we are a country awakened to danger and called to defend freedom. Our grief has turned to anger, and anger to resolution. Whether we bring our enemies to justice, or bring justice to our enemies, justice will be done. (Applause.)

I thank the Congress for its leadership at such an important time. All of America was touched on the evening of the tragedy to see Republicans and Democrats joined together on the steps of this Capitol, singing "God Bless America." And you did more than sing; you acted, by delivering $40 billion to rebuild our communities and meet the needs of our military.

Speaker Hastert, Minority Leader Gephardt, Majority Leader Daschle and Senator Lott, I thank you for your friendship, for your leadership and for your service to our country. (Applause.)

And on behalf of the American people, I thank the world for its outpouring of support. America will never forget the sounds of our National Anthem playing at Buckingham Palace, on the streets of Paris, and at Berlin's Brandenburg Gate.

We will not forget South Korean children gathering to pray outside our embassy in Seoul, or the prayers of sympathy offered at a mosque in Cairo. We will not forget moments of silence and days of mourning in Australia and Africa and Latin America.

Nor will we forget the citizens of 80 other nations who died with our own: dozens of Pakistanis; more than 130 Israelis; more than 250 citizens of India; men and women from El Salvador, Iran, Mexico and Japan; and hundreds of British citizens. America has no truer friend than Great Britain. (Applause.) Once again, we are joined together in a great cause—so honored the British Prime Minister has crossed an ocean to show his unity of purpose with America. Thank you for coming, friend. (Applause.)

On September the 11th, enemies of freedom committed an act of war against our country. Americans have known wars—but for the past 136 years, they have been wars on foreign soil, except for one Sunday in 1941. Americans have known the casualties of war—but not at the center of a great city on a peaceful morning. Americans have known surprise attacks—but never before on thousands of civilians. All of this was brought upon us in a single day—and night fell on a different world, a world where freedom itself is under attack.

Americans have many questions tonight. Americans are asking: Who attacked our country? The evidence we have gathered all points to a collection of loosely affiliated terrorist organizations known as al Qaeda. They are the same murderers indicted for bombing American embassies in Tanzania and Kenya, and responsible for bombing the USS Cole.

Al Qaeda is to terror what the mafia is to crime. But its goal is not making money; its goal is remaking the world—and imposing its radical beliefs on people everywhere.

The terrorists practice a fringe form of Islamic extremism that has been rejected by Muslim scholars and the vast majority of Muslim clerics—a fringe movement that perverts the peaceful teachings of Islam. The terrorists' directive commands them to kill Christians and Jews, to kill all Americans, and make no distinction among military and civilians, including women and children.

This group and its leader—a person named Osama bin Laden—are linked to many other organizations in different countries, including the Egyptian Islamic Jihad and the Islamic Movement of Uzbekistan. There are thousands of these terrorists in more than 60 countries. They are recruited from their own nations and neighborhoods and brought to camps in places like Afghanistan, where they are trained in the tactics of terror. They are sent back to their homes or sent to hide in countries around the world to plot evil and destruction.

The leadership of al Qaeda has great influence in Afghanistan and supports the Taliban regime in controlling most of that country. In Afghanistan, we see al Qaeda's vision for the world.

Afghanistan's people have been brutalized—many are starving and many have fled. Women are not allowed to attend school. You can be jailed for owning a television. Religion can be practiced only as their leaders dictate. A man can be jailed in Afghanistan if his beard is not long enough.

The United States respects the people of Afghanistan—after all, we are currently its largest source of humanitarian aid—but we condemn the Taliban regime. (Applause.) It is not only repressing its own people, it is threatening people everywhere by sponsoring and sheltering and supplying terrorists. By aiding and abetting murder, the Taliban regime is committing murder.

And tonight, the United States of America makes the following demands on the Taliban: Deliver to United States authorities all the leaders of al Qaeda who hide in your land. (Applause.) Release all foreign nationals, including American citizens, you have unjustly imprisoned. Protect foreign journalists, diplomats and aid workers in your country. Close immediately and permanently every terrorist training camp in Afghanistan, and hand over every terrorist, and every person in their support structure, to appropriate authorities. (Applause.) Give the United States full access to terrorist training camps, so we can make sure they are no longer operating.

These demands are not open to negotiation or discussion. (Applause.) The Taliban must act, and act immediately. They will hand over the terrorists, or they will share in their fate.

I also want to speak tonight directly to Muslims throughout the world. We respect your faith. It's practiced freely by many millions of Americans, and by millions more in countries that America counts as friends. Its teachings are good and peaceful, and those who commit evil in the name of Allah blaspheme the name of Allah. (Applause.) The terrorists are traitors to their own faith, trying, in effect, to hijack Islam itself. The enemy of America is not our many Muslim friends; it is not our many Arab friends. Our enemy is a radical network of terrorists, and every government that supports them. (Applause.)

Our war on terror begins with al Qaeda, but it does not end there. It will not end until every terrorist group of global reach has been found, stopped and defeated. (Applause.)

Americans are asking, why do they hate us? They hate what we see right here in this chamber—a democratically elected government. Their leaders are self-appointed. They hate our freedoms—our freedom of religion, our freedom of speech, our freedom to vote and assemble and disagree with each other.

They want to overthrow existing governments in many Muslim countries, such as Egypt, Saudi Arabia, and Jordan. They want to drive Israel out of the Middle East. They want to drive Christians and Jews out of vast regions of Asia and Africa.

These terrorists kill not merely to end lives, but to disrupt and end a way of life. With every atrocity, they hope that America grows fearful, retreating from the world and forsaking our friends. They stand against us, because we stand in their way.

We are not deceived by their pretenses to piety. We have seen their kind before. They are the heirs of all the murderous ideologies of the 20th century. By sacrificing human life to serve their radical visions—by abandoning every value except the will to power—they follow in the path of fascism, and Nazism, and totalitarianism. And they will follow that path all the way, to where it ends: in history's unmarked grave of discarded lies. (Applause.)

Americans are asking: How will we fight and win this war? We will direct every resource at our command—every means of diplomacy, every tool of intelligence, every instrument of law enforcement, every financial influence, and every necessary weapon of war—to the disruption and to the defeat of the global terror network.

This war will not be like the war against Iraq a decade ago, with a decisive liberation of territory and a swift conclusion. It will not look like the air war above Kosovo two years ago, where no ground troops were used and not a single American was lost in combat.

Our response involves far more than instant retaliation and isolated strikes. Americans should not expect one battle, but a lengthy campaign, unlike any other we have ever seen. It may include dramatic strikes, visible on TV, and covert operations, secret even in success. We will starve terrorists of funding, turn them one against another, drive them from place to place, until there is no refuge or no rest. And we will pursue nations that provide aid or safe haven to terrorism. Every nation, in every region, now has a decision to make. Either you are with us, or you are with the terrorists. (Applause.) From this day forward, any nation that continues to harbor or support terrorism will be regarded by the United States as a hostile regime.

Our nation has been put on notice: We are not immune from attack. We will take defensive measures against terrorism to protect Americans. Today, dozens of federal departments and agencies, as well as state and local governments, have responsibilities affecting homeland security. These efforts must be coordinated at the highest level. So tonight I announce the creation of a Cabinet-level position reporting directly to me—the Office of Homeland Security.

And tonight I also announce a distinguished American to lead this effort, to strengthen American security: a military veteran, an effective governor, a true patriot, a trusted friend—Pennsylvania's Tom Ridge. (Applause.) He will lead, oversee and coordinate a comprehensive national strategy to safeguard our country against terrorism, and respond to any attacks that may come.

These measures are essential. But the only way to defeat terrorism as a threat to our way of life is to stop it, eliminate it, and destroy it where it grows. (Applause.)

Many will be involved in this effort, from FBI agents to intelligence operatives to the reservists we have called to active duty. All deserve our thanks, and all have our prayers. And tonight, a few miles from the damaged Pentagon, I have a message for our military: Be ready. I've called the Armed Forces to alert, and there is a reason. The hour is coming when America will act, and you will make us proud. (Applause.)

This is not, however, just America's fight. And what is at stake is not just America's freedom. This is the world's fight. This is civilization's fight. This is the fight of all who believe in progress and pluralism, tolerance and freedom.

We ask every nation to join us. We will ask, and we will need, the help of police forces, intelligence services, and banking systems around the world. The United States is grateful that many nations and many international organizations have already responded—with sympathy and with support. Nations from Latin America, to Asia, to Africa, to Europe, to the Islamic world. Perhaps the NATO Charter reflects best the attitude of the world: An attack on one is an attack on all.

The civilized world is rallying to America's side. They understand that if this terror goes unpunished, their own cities, their own citizens may be next. Terror, unanswered, can not only bring down buildings, it can threaten the stability of legitimate governments. And you know what—we're not going to allow it. (Applause.)

Americans are asking: What is expected of us? I ask you to live your lives, and hug your children. I know many citizens have fears tonight, and I ask you to be calm and resolute, even in the face of a continuing threat.

I ask you to uphold the values of America, and remember why so many have come here. We are in a fight for our principles, and our first responsibility is to live by them. No one should be singled out for unfair treatment or unkind words because of their ethnic background or religious faith. (Applause.)

I ask you to continue to support the victims of this tragedy with your contributions. Those who want to give can go to a central source of information, libertyunites.org, to find the names of groups providing direct help in New York, Pennsylvania, and Virginia.

The thousands of FBI agents who are now at work in this investigation may need your cooperation, and I ask you to give it.

I ask for your patience, with the delays and inconveniences that may accompany tighter security; and for your patience in what will be a long struggle.

I ask your continued participation and confidence in the American economy. Terrorists attacked a symbol of American prosperity. They did not touch its source. America is successful because of the hard work, and creativity, and enterprise of our people. These were the true strengths of our economy before September 11th, and they are our strengths today. (Applause.)

And, finally, please continue praying for the victims of terror and their families, for those in uniform, and for our great country. Prayer has comforted us in sorrow, and will help strengthen us for the journey ahead.

Tonight I thank my fellow Americans for what you have already done and for what you will do. And ladies and gentlemen of the Congress, I thank you, their representatives, for what you have already done and for what we will do together.

Tonight, we face new and sudden national challenges. We will come together to improve air safety, to dramatically expand the number of air marshals on domestic flights, and take new measures to prevent hijacking. We will come together to promote stability and keep our airlines flying, with direct assistance during this emergency. (Applause.)

We will come together to give law enforcement the additional tools it needs to track down terror here at home. (Applause.) We will come together to strengthen our intelligence capabilities to know the plans of terrorists before they act, and find them before they strike. (Applause.)

We will come together to take active steps that strengthen America's economy, and put our people back to work.

Tonight we welcome two leaders who embody the extraordinary spirit of all New Yorkers: Governor George Pataki, and Mayor Rudolph Giuliani. (Applause.) As a symbol of America's resolve, my administration will work with Congress, and these two leaders, to show the world that we will rebuild New York City. (Applause.)

After all that has just passed—all the lives taken, and all the possibilities and hopes that died with them—it is natural to wonder if America's future is one of fear. Some speak of an age of terror. I know there are struggles ahead, and dangers to face. But this country will define our times, not be defined by them. As long as the United States of America is determined and strong, this will not be an age of terror; this will be an age of liberty, here and across the world. (Applause.)

Great harm has been done to us. We have suffered great loss. And in our grief and anger we have found our mission and our moment. Freedom and fear are at war. The advance of human freedom—the great achievement of our time, and the great hope of every time—now depends on us. Our nation—this generation—will lift a dark threat of violence from our people and our future. We will rally the world to this cause by our efforts, by our courage. We will not tire, we will not falter, and we will not fail. (Applause.)

It is my hope that in the months and years ahead, life will return almost to normal. We'll go back to our lives and routines, and that is good. Even grief recedes with time and grace. But our resolve must not pass. Each of us will remember what happened that day, and to whom it happened. We'll remember the moment the news came—where we were and what we were doing. Some will remember an image of a fire, or a story of rescue. Some will carry memories of a face and a voice gone forever.

And I will carry this: It is the police shield of a man named George Howard, who died at the World Trade Center trying to save others. It was given to me by his mom, Arlene, as a proud memorial to her son. This is my reminder of lives that ended, and a task that does not end. (Applause.)

I will not forget this wound to our country or those who inflicted it. I will not yield; I will not rest; I will not relent in waging this struggle for freedom and security for the American people.

The course of this conflict is not known, yet its outcome is certain. Freedom and fear, justice and cruelty, have always been at war, and we know that God is not neutral between them. (Applause.)

Fellow citizens, we'll meet violence with patient justice—assured of the rightness of our cause, and confident of the victories to come. In all that lies before us, may God grant us wisdom, and may He watch over the United States of America.

Thank you. (Applause.)

http://www.whitehouse.gov/news/releases/2001/09/20010920-8.html

## ADDRESS BY THE PRESIDENT OF THE UNITED STATES

December 8, 1941

To the Congress of the United States:

Yesterday, December 7, 1941—a date which will live in infamy—the United States of America was suddenly and deliberately attacked by naval and air forces of the Empire of Japan.

The United States was at peace with that nation and, at the solicitation of Japan, was still in conversation with the government and its emperor looking toward the maintenance of peace in the Pacific.

Indeed, one hour after Japanese air squadrons had commenced bombing in Oahu, the Japanese ambassador to the United States and his colleagues delivered to the Secretary of State a formal reply to a recent American message. While this reply stated that it seemed useless to continue the existing diplomatic negotiations, it contained no threat or hint of war or armed attack.

It will be recorded that the distance of Hawaii from Japan makes it obvious that the attack was deliberately planned many days or even weeks ago. During the intervening time, the Japanese government has deliberately sought to deceive the United States by false statements and expressions of hope for continued peace.

The attack yesterday on the Hawaiian islands has caused severe damage to American naval and military forces. Very many American lives have been lost. In addition, American ships have been reported torpedoed on the high seas between San Francisco and Honolulu.

Yesterday, the Japanese government also launched an attack against Malaya.

Last night, Japanese forces attacked Hong Kong.

Last night, Japanese forces attacked Guam.

Last night, Japanese forces attacked the Philippine Islands.

Last night, the Japanese attacked Wake Island.

This morning, the Japanese attacked Midway Island.

Japan has, therefore, undertaken a surprise offensive extending throughout the Pacific area. The facts of yesterday speak for themselves. The people of the United States have already formed their opinions and well understand the implications to the very life and safety of our nation.

As commander in chief of the Army and Navy, I have directed that all measures be taken for our defense.

Always will we remember the character of the onslaught against us.

No matter how long it may take us to overcome this premeditated invasion, the American people in their righteous might will win through to absolute victory.

I believe I interpret the will of the Congress and of the people when I assert that we will not only defend ourselves to the uttermost, but will make very certain that this form of treachery shall never endanger us again.

Hostilities exist. There is no blinking at the fact that that our people, our territory and our interests are in grave danger.

With confidence in our armed forces—with the unbounding determination of our people—we will gain the inevitable triumph—so help us God.

I ask that the Congress declare that since the unprovoked and dastardly attack by Japan on Sunday, December 7, a state of war has existed between the United States and the Japanese empire.

Franklin D. Roosevelt
http://bcn.boulder.co.us/government/national/speeches/spch2.html

## ADDRESS OF THE PRESIDENT
## BROADCAST FROM THE OVAL ROOM OF THE
## WHITE HOUSE, NATIONALLY, AND OVER A
## WORLD-WIDE HOOKUP

December 9, 1941 10:00 p.m.

My fellow Americans:

The sudden criminal attacks perpetrated by the Japanese in the Pacific provide the climax of a decade of international immorality.

Powerful and resourceful gangsters have banded together to make war upon the whole human race. Their challenge has now been flung at the United States of America. The Japanese have treacherously violated the longstanding peace between us. Many American soldiers and sailors have been killed by enemy action. American ships have been sunk; American airplanes have been destroyed.

The Congress and the people of the United States have accepted that challenge.

Together with other free peoples, we are now fighting to maintain our right to live among our world neighbors in freedom, in common decency, without fear of assault.

I have prepared the full record of our past relations with Japan, and it will be submitted to the Congress. It begins with the visit of Commodore Parry to Japan eighty-eight years ago. It ends with the visit of two Japanese emissaries to the Secretary of State last Sunday, an hour after Japanese forces had loosed their bombs and machine guns against our flag, our forces and our citizens.

I can say with utmost confidence that no Americans today or a thousand years hence, need feel anything but pride in our patience and in our efforts through all the years toward achieving a peace in the Pacific which would be fair and honorable to every nation, large or small. And no honest person, today or a thousand years hence, will be able to suppress a sense of indignation and horror at the treachery committed by the military dictators of Japan, under the very shadow of the flag of peace borne by their special envoys in our midst.

The course that Japan has followed for the past ten years in Asia has paralleled the course of Hitler and Mussolini in Europe and in Africa. Today, it has become far more than a parallel. It is actual collaboration so well calculated that all the continents of the world, and all the oceans, are now considered by the Axis strategists as one gigantic battlefield.

In 1931, ten years ago, Japan invaded Manchukuo—without warning.

In 1935, Italy invaded Ethiopia—without warning. In 1938, Hitler occupied Austria—without warning.

In 1939, Hitler invaded Czechoslovakia—without warning. Later in '39, Hitler invaded Poland—without warning. In 1940, Hitler invaded Norway, Denmark, the Netherlands, Belgium and Luxembourg—without warning.

In 1940, Italy attacked France and later Greece—without warning.

And this year, in 1941, the Axis Powers attacked Yugoslavia and Greece and they dominated the Balkans—without warning. In 1941, also, Hitler invaded Russia—without warning. And now Japan has attacked Malaya and Thailand—and the United States—without warning.

It is all of one pattern.

We are now in this war. We are all in it—all the way. Every single man, woman and child is a partner in the most tremendous undertaking of our American history. We must share together the bad news and the good news, the defeats and the victories—the changing fortunes of war.

So far, the news has been all bad. We have suffered a serious setback in Hawaii. Our forces in the Philippines, which include the brave people of that Commonwealth, are taking punishment, but are defending themselves vigorously. The reports from Guam and Wake and Midway Islands are still confused, but we must be prepared for the announcement that all these three outposts have been seized.

The casualty lists of these first few days will undoubtedly be large. I deeply feel the anxiety of all of the families of the men in our armed forces and the relatives of people in cities which have been bombed. I can only give them my solemn promise that they will get news just as quickly as possible.

This Government will put its trust in the stamina of the American people, and will give the facts to the public just as soon as two conditions have been fulfilled: first, that the information has been definitely and officially confirmed; and, second, that the release of the information at the time it is received will not prove valuable to the enemy directly or indirectly.

Most earnestly I urge my countrymen to reject all rumors. These ugly little hints of complete disaster fly thick and fast in wartime. They have to be examined and appraised.

As an example, I can tell you frankly that until further surveys are made, I have not sufficient information to state the exact damage which has been done to our naval vessels at Pearl Harbor. Admittedly the damage is serious. But no one can say how serious, until we know how much of this damage can be repaired and how quickly the necessary repairs can be made.

I cite as another example a statement made on Sunday night that a Japanese carrier had been located and sunk off the Canal Zone. And when you hear statements that are attributed to what they call "an authoritative source," you can be reasonably sure from now on that under these war circumstances the "authoritative source" is not any person in authority.

Many rumors and reports which we now hear originate, of course, with enemy sources. For instance, today the Japanese are claiming that as a result of their one action against Hawaii they have gained naval supremacy in the Pacific. This is an old trick of propaganda which has been used innumerable times by the Nazis. The purposes of such fantastic claims are, of course, to spread fear and confusion among us, and to goad us into revealing military information which our enemies are desperately anxious to obtain.

Our Government will not be caught in this obvious trap—and neither will the people of the United States.

It must be remembered by each and every one of us that our free and rapid communication these days must be greatly restricted in wartime. It is not possible to receive full and speedy and accurate reports from distant areas of combat. This is particularly true where naval operations are concerned. For in these days of the marvels of the radio it is often impossible for the Commanders of various units to report their activities by radio at all, for the very simple reason that this information would become available to the enemy and would disclose their position and their plan of defense or attack.

Of necessity there will be delays in officially confirming or denying reports of operations, but we will not hide facts from the country if we know the facts and if the enemy will not be aided by their disclosure.

To all newspapers and radio stations—all those who reach the eyes and ears of the American people—I say this: You have a most grave responsibility to the nation now and for the duration of this war.

If you feel that your Government is not disclosing enough of the truth, you have every right to say so. But in the absence of all the facts, as revealed by official sources, you have no right in the ethics of patriotism to deal out unconfirmed reports in such a way as to make people believe that they are gospel truth. Every citizen, in every walk of life, shares this same responsibility. The lives of our soldiers and sailors—the whole future of this nation—depend upon the manner in which each and every one of us fulfills his obligation to our country. Now a word about the recent past and the future. A year and a half has elapsed since the fall of France, when the whole world first realized the mechanized might which the Axis nations had been building up for so many years. America has used that year and a half to great advantage. Knowing that the attack might reach us in all too short a time, we immediately began greatly to increase our industrial strength and our capacity to meet the demands of modern warfare.

Precious months were gained by sending vast quantities of our war material to the nations of the world still able to resist Axis aggression. Our policy rested on the fundamental truth that the defense of any country resisting Hitler or Japan was in the long run the defense of our own country. That policy has been justified. It has given us time, invaluable time, to build our American assembly lines of production.

Assembly lines are now in operation. Others are being rushed to completion. A steady stream of tanks and planes, of guns and ships and shells and equipment—that is what these eighteen months have given us.

But it is all only a beginning of what still has to be done. We must be set to face a long war against crafty and powerful bandits. The attack at Pearl Harbor can be repeated at any one of many points, points in both oceans and along both our coast lines and against all the rest of the Hemisphere.

It will not only be a long war, it will be a hard war. That is the basis on which we now lay all our plans. That is the yardstick by which we measure what we shall need and demand; money, materials, doubled and quadrupled production—ever-increasing. The production must be not only for our own Army and Navy and air forces. It must reinforce the other armies and navies and air forces fighting the Nazis and the war lords of Japan throughout the Americas and throughout the world. I have been working today on the subject of production. Your Government has decided on two broad policies.

The first is to speed up all existing production by working on a seven day week basis in every war industry, including the production of essential raw materials.

The second policy, now being put into form, is to rush additions to the capacity of production by building more new plants, by adding to old plants, and by using the many smaller plants for war needs.

Over the hard road of the past months, we have at times met obstacles and difficulties, divisions and disputes, indifference and callousness. That is now all past—and, I am sure, forgotten.

The fact is that the country now has an organization in Washington built around men and women who are recognized experts in their own fields. I think the country knows that the people who are actually responsible in each and every one of these many fields are pulling together with a teamwork that has never before been excelled.

On the road ahead there lies hard work—gruelling work—day and night, every hour and every minute.

I was about to add that ahead there lies sacrifice for all of us.

But it is not correct to use that word. The United States does not consider it a sacrifice to do all one can, to give one's best to our nation, when the nation is fighting for its existence and its future life.

It is not a sacrifice for any man, old or young, to be in the Army or the Navy of the United States. Rather it is a privilege.

It is not a sacrifice for the industrialist or the wage earner, the farmer or the shopkeeper, the trainmen or the doctor, to pay more taxes, to buy more bonds, to forego extra profits, to work longer or harder at the task for which he is best fitted. Rather it is a privilege.

It is not a sacrifice to do without many things to which we are accustomed if the national defense calls for doing without it.

A review this morning leads me to the conclusion that at present we shall not have to curtail the normal use of articles of food. There is enough food today for all of us and enough left over to send to those who are fighting on the same side with us.

But there will be a clear and definite shortage of metals for many kinds of civilian use, for the very good reason that in our increased program we shall need for war purposes more than half of that portion of the principal metals which during the past year have gone into articles for civilian use. Yes, we shall have to give up many things entirely.

And I am sure that the people in every part of the nation are prepared in their individual living to win this war. I am sure that they will cheerfully help to pay a large part of its financial cost while it goes on. I am sure they will cheerfully give up those material things that they are asked to give up. And I am sure that they will retain all those great spiritual things without which we cannot win through.

I repeat that the United States can accept no result save victory, final and complete. Not only must the shame of Japanese treachery be wiped out, but the sources of international brutality, wherever they exist, must be absolutely and finally broken.

In my Message to the Congress yesterday I said that we "will make very certain that this form of treachery shall never endanger us again." In order to achieve that certainty, we must begin the great task that is before us by abandoning once and for all the illusion that we can ever again isolate ourselves from the rest of humanity.

In these past few years—and, most violently, in the past three days—we have learned a terrible lesson.

It is our obligation to our dead—it is our sacred obligation to their children and to our children—that we must never forget what we have learned.

And what we have learned is this:

There is no such thing as security for any nation—or any individual—in a world ruled by the principles of gangsterism. There is no such thing as impregnable defense against powerful aggressors who sneak up in the dark and strike without warning.

We have learned that our ocean-girt hemisphere is not immune from severe attack—that we cannot measure our safety in terms of miles on any map any more.

We may acknowledge that our enemies have performed a brilliant feat of deception, perfectly timed and executed with great skill. It was a thoroughly dishonorable deed, but we must face the fact that modern warfare as conducted in the Nazi manner is a dirty business. We don't like it—we didn't want to get in it—but we are in it and we're going to fight it with everything we've got.

I do not think any American has any doubt of our ability to administer proper punishment to the perpetrators of these crimes. Your Government knows that for weeks Germany has been telling Japan that if Japan did not attack the United States, Japan would not share in dividing the spoils with Germany when peace came. She was promised by Germany that if she came in she would receive the complete and perpetual control of the whole of the Pacific area—and that means not only the Ear East, but also all of the Islands in the Pacific, and also a stranglehold on the west coast of North, Central and South America. We know also that Germany and Japan are conducting their military and naval operations in accordance with a joint plan. That plan considers all peoples and nations which are not helping the Axis powers as common enemies of each and every one of the Axis powers.

That is their simple and obvious grand strategy. And that is why the American people must realize that it can be matched only with similar grand strategy. We must realize for example that Japanese successes against the United States in the Pacific are helpful to German operations in Libya; that any German success against the Caucasus is inevitably an assistance to Japan in her operations against the Dutch East Indies; that a German attack against Algiers or Morocco opens the way to a German attack against South America and the Canal.

On the other side of the picture, we must learn also to know that guerilla warfare against the Germans in, let us say Serbia or Norway, helps us; that a successful Russian offensive against the Germans helps us; and that British successes on land or sea in any part of the world strengthen our hands.

Remember always that Germany and Italy, regardless of any formal declaration of war, consider themselves at war with the United States at this moment just as much as they consider themselves at war with Britain or Russia. And Germany puts all the other Republics of the Americas into the same category of enemies. The people of our sister Republics of this Hemisphere can be honored by that fact.

The true goal we seek is far above and beyond the ugly field of battle. When we resort to force, as now we must, we are determined that this force shall be directed toward ultimate good as well as against immediate evil. We Americans are not destroyers—we are builders.

We are now in the midst of a war, not for conquest, not for vengeance, but for a world in which this nation, and all that this nation represents, will be safe for our children. We expect to eliminate the danger from Japan, but it would serve us ill if we accomplished that and found that the rest of the world was dominated by Hitler and Mussolini.

So we are going to win the war and we are going to win the peace that follows.

And in the difficult hours of this day—through dark days that may be yet to come—we will know that the vast majority of the members of the human race are on our side. Many of them are fighting with us. All of them are praying for us. But, in representing our cause, we represent theirs as well—our hope and their hope for liberty under God.

http://www.mhric.org/fdr/chat19.html

## NOTES

1 Richard E. Neustadt, *Presidential Power: The Politics of Leadership from FDR to Carter,* New York: John Wiley, 1980, p. 10. Originally published in 1960.
2 Walter Laqueur, *Terrorism,* Boston: Little, Brown, 1977, p. 109. Cited in Steven Livingston, *The Terrorism Spectacle,* Boulder: Westview Press, 1994, p. 2.
3 Cited in Steven Livingston, *The Terrorism Spectacle,* Boulder: Westview Press, 1994, p. 3. For more on this symbiosis, see M. Cherif Bassiouni, "Problems of Media Coverage of Nonstate-Sponsored Terror-Violence Incidents," in L.Z. Freedman and Yonah Alexander (Eds.), *Perspectives on Terrorism,* Wilmington, DE: Scholarly Resources, 1983.
4 For a discussion of these issues, see Livingston.
5 The discussion in this paragraph is largely taken from Roderick P. Hart, *Verbal Style and the Presidency: A Computer-Based Analysis,* Orlando: Academic Press, 1984, pp. 2–5.
6 Craig Allen Smith and Kathy B. Smith, *The White House Speaks: Presidential Leadership as Persuasion,* Westport, CT: Praeger, 1994, p. 21.
7 Livingston, p. 178.
8 Available at www.whitehouse.gov/news/releases/2001/09/20010911.html.
9 Available at www.whitehouse.gov/news/releases/2001/09/20010911-10.html.
10 Hart, p. 61.
11 John Wilson, *Politically Speaking: The Pragmatic Analysis of Political Language,* Oxford, Basil Blackwell, 1990, p. 59.
12 Available at www.whitehouse.gov/news/releases/2001/09/20010911-1.html.
13 Available at www.whitehouse.gov/news/releases/2001/09/20010911-16.html.
14 Benedict Anderson, *Imagined Communities,* London: Verso, 1983, p. 6.
15 Lauren Berlant, *The Anatomy of National Fantasy: Hawthorne, Utopia, and Everyday Life,* Chicago: University of Chicago Press, 1991, p. 4.
16 Berlant, p. 193.
17 Smith and Smith, p. 79.
18 Available at www.number-10.gov.uk/news.asp?NewId=2545.
19 Ibid.
20 Hart, pp. 42–44.
21 Hart, pp. 45–46.
22 Karlyn Kohrs Campbell and Kathleen Hall Jamieson, *Deeds Done in Words: Presidential Rhetoric and Genres of Governance,* Chicago: University of Chicago Press, 1990, p. 118.
23 Ibid, p. 105.
24 Available at www.whitehouse.gov/news/releases/2001/09/20010920-8.html.
25 Available at www.whitehouse.gov/news/releases/2001/10/20011007-8.html.
26 Available at www.ibiblio.org/pha/77-1-148/77-1-148.html.
27 Available at www.mhric.org/fdr/chat19.html.

# 2

# Becoming President

Part of being the president is being the nation's chaplain.
　　Leon Panetta, White House chief of staff for President Clinton

Before September 11, George W. Bush's presumed inadequacies and his status as America's first appointed president were fair game. From satirical television to published accounts, irreverent reminders of Bush's thin resume were ubiquitous. *Is Our Children Learning: The Case Against Prezident George W. Bush* was typical. In it, political analyst Paul Begala summarizes the basis for skepticism:

> The guy who got into Yale despite being an underachieving party boy, the guy who got into the Texas Air National Guard despite scoring in the bottom 25 percent of the pilot aptitude test, the guy who got into the oil business despite not knowing a dry hole from a dry martini, the guy who got into the owners' box of the Texas Rangers despite owning less than 2 percent of the team, the guy who got into the multimillionaires' club despite being a failure in business now gets into the White House despite losing the election.[1]

Harvard Law Professor Alan Dershowitz offered a highbrow complaint in *Supreme Injustice: How the High Court Hijacked Election 2000*.[2] The subtitle holds a terrible irony for an account that warns against the loss of liberty within America's judicial system. The dangers to civil liberties in the wake of 9/11 trump Dershowitz's earlier call for concern. But these new dangers became possible only within the context of a popularly accepted

Bush presidency. And it was neither popular nor entirely accepted at its outset. When Bush was chosen as *Time* magazine's "Man of the Year" in December 2000, the lack of acceptance was underscored:

> For the proud son of a one-term President, could there be a more humbling path to power than this? The candidate with the perfect bloodlines comes to office amid charges that his is a bastard presidency, sired not by the voters but by the courts. ... Bush rose last Wednesday night with tears in his eyes and promised, "I will work to earn your respect," all but admitting it does not just come with the job when you win this way. ... [W]hile the office has at last been won, the honor remains to be earned.[3]

The previous chapter detailed the rhetorical journey that accompanied George W. Bush's ascendance to commander in chief during "America's New War." But it was more than his military role that transformed a persistent focus of cultural humor into the president of the United States, with soaring approval ratings. This chapter explores another rhetorical turning point: the events of September 14, 2001. On that National Day of Prayer and Remembrance, the president addressed the nation at services in the National Cathedral, then visited "ground zero" in New York City.

## A NATIONAL CATHEDRAL

The physical context of the cathedral embodies American tensions around the separation of church and state, and around privilege versus inclusion. Notwithstanding the First Amendment's prohibition of a congressional "establishment of religion," the church was chartered by Congress in 1893 as a national cathedral. One might say, using a term from the previous chapter, it is a "national symbolic site"—in this case, a location where government, religion, culture, and the military coalesce, sometimes in uneasy contradiction. This tension is reflected in the words of the cathedral's Dean, the Very Reverend Nathan D. Baxter, in April 2001:

> The question is often asked of me. ... "How can you be a House of Prayer for All People when you are a Christian church?" What makes it national to many is that within the Cathedral's art and

craft is presented the broad expanse of our national life. The Cathedral's stained-glass windows, wood and stone carving, metal work, extensive needlepoint and other art is the history of our nation—its struggles for independence and civil rights; its military conflicts; its achievements in fields such as religion science, law, politics, medicine and civics; and the great heroes of our history.[4]

George Bush, Sr. was even more explicit in the conflation of state and church when he spoke at the church's dedication ceremony in 1990. Below are several excerpts from his remarks.[5]

- The cathedral was, he told the audience, "not just a church [but] a house of prayer for a nation, built on the rock of religious faith, a nation we celebrate as 'one nation under God'."
- "We have constructed here this symbol of our nation's spiritual life, overlooking the center of our nation's secular life."
- Quoting President Woodrow Wilson, he said, "Our civilization cannot survive materially unless it be redeemed spiritually." And in his own words, "to do that we must govern by the imperatives of a strong moral compass ... a compass oriented to the words of St. Paul. ..."
- This is, he told the assembled, "a cathedral that's not just about faith but was also about a nation and its people: a cathedral where mosaics of the Great Seal of the United States and the State seals are set into the floors ... where needlepoint memorials are to Herman Melville, Alexander Graham Bell, Harriet Tubman, where lie the graves of President Wilson, Admiral George Dewey, and Helen Keller; where the mesmerizing stained-glass Space Window includes a Moon rock given by astronaut Michael Collins, who went to school on these very grounds. ... It's a place where the history of the cathedral and the country have been interwoven." Ironically, this would aptly describe the role of Westminster Abbey, the seat of Britain's official church. And, I hope to show below, at least metaphorically, that George W. Bush came to the National Cathedral on September 14 for a coronation of sorts.
- In 1990, his father implicitly defined America in terms of a direct lineage from state to church, from Congress to the cathedral: he

informed the audience that the laying of the cornerstone in 1907 "was a very American ceremony, President Teddy Roosevelt spoke, and Bishop Satterlee tapped the stone with the gavel which George Washington had used to set the cornerstone of the United States Capitol."

The cathedral is an enormous and beautiful edifice, worthy of state occasions. Within the United States only Saint John's in New York City is larger. And, to be fair, the cathedral has always been conceived as an ecumenical institution, "a national house of prayer for all people."[6] First imagined under the presidency of George Washington, it was proposed as a church "intended for national purposes, such as public prayer, thanksgiving, funeral orations, etc., and assigned to the special use of no particular Sect or denomination, but equally open to all."[7]

At the same time, the cathedral is certainly a nationally sanctioned Christian church (formally the Cathedral Church of Saint Peter and Saint Paul). What makes it "a church for all people," Dean Baxtor explains, is "the welcoming Spirit of Christ."[8] And it is indeed sectarian; it serves as the seat of two Episcopal bishops: the Presiding Bishop of the Episcopal Church USA and the Episcopal Bishop of Washington. Its Episcopal status stands as a reminder of America's historical ties to Britain. When the foundation stone was laid in 1907, the Bishop of London spoke. When the nave was dedicated in 1976, the ceremonies were attended by the Queen of England and the Archbishop of Canterbury.

To designate an Episcopal church as the National Cathedral risks reifying the social privilege of largely well-to-do, white, Anglo-Saxon Protestants. In his 1990 remarks, George Bush, Sr. claims the church as his own, "Our personal family compass has for many years led us here for public and private worship. We were neighbors when we lived in the Vice President's residence, and before that our children went to school at St. Alban's [the cathedral's college preparatory school for boys]. I was a board member at the National Cathedral School [the girl's school], and Canon Martin baptized one of our grandchildren, and two sons were confirmed here." Indeed, George W. Bush, son of privilege, could be said to be coming home on September 14 when he entered the church.

But to dismiss the inclusive nature of the institution would be to do it a serious disservice. Today, the Bishop of Washington is an Anglo woman (Jane Holmes Dixon), and the church's Dean (Nathan Baxter) is an African American man. The church's Web site announces that "on March 31, 1968, the Rev. Dr. Martin Luther King, Jr., preached his last Sunday sermon at the Cathedral. A memorial service for King was held in the Cathedral five days later."[9] The tension between privilege and inclusion, sectarianism and ecumenism was visible in the September 14 prayer service.

## A NATIONAL EVENT

The event was constructed simultaneously by those who chose the participants (significantly the president and first lady), by the speakers themselves, by the news commentators who continually framed the event for the viewing public, and by the visual framing provided by national and local networks. For example, throughout most of the broadcast three (national) subheadings appeared simultaneously on the lower left of my screen:

ABC NEWS LIVE COVERAGE

NATIONAL CATHEDRAL

DAY OF PRAYER AND REMEMBRANCE

Occasionally, these would surmount subtitles provided by the local station. And, while one read these, a speaker or newscaster might be talking.

Although these multiple perspectives were not always parallel, they were never at cross-purposes. In the end, the multi-layered presentation worked to unite political, religious, and cultural strands in support of a Bush presidency and the policies it would undertake. In the discussion that follows, I will be quoting from the broadcast coverage of ABC News, including the commentary of Canadian-born news anchor Peter Jennings. For more than a decade he has been the most-watched evening newscaster in America.

The Jennings commentary went a long way in defining the event. Early on, in the context of the musical prelude, Jennings framed the moment: "The U.S. **Army** Orchestra, organized in the 1950s to meet requirements just such as this—great **national occasions**, great **state occasions** in Washington when music as we hear there in the playing of '**America** the Beautiful' and '**God** Bless America' are so essential to occasions such as this." As I indicate in bold, "occasions such as this" are apparently simultaneously national, military, and religious. Jennings underscored the religious nature of an event specifically sanctioned by the president: "Everybody is now in place for this national prayer service and as we said the President and Mrs. Bush have had a very specific hand in putting it together." Jennings reminded the audience that within this moment of prayer, they were witnessing the convening of the nation's power elite. "This is an invited audience, it is not open to the public. What you are seeing in bits and pieces is the political and military and to some extent the bureaucratic superstructure of the country." Most living former presidents attended along with government, military, and religious leaders.

From the perspective of the Bushes, it was both a local and national religious moment. Jennings reported, "President Bush had a hand along with Mrs. Bush in planning the particulars of this service and one of the people who will preach today will be the great and close friend of his from Texas, Kirbyjon Caldwell from the Windsor Village United Methodist church there ... all of this very close to the Bush family and to the national family."

As "the national family" watched, it's fair to observe that, initially, George W. Bush was visually eclipsed. Presumably for reasons of both security and perhaps protocol, he arrived at the last possible moment and hurried to his seat. He had already been upstaged. The camera has always loved the Clintons, and it had spent more than five minutes gazing on the former first family, with occasional forays to other notables and to ground zero and Union Square in New York City. The news commentator Jennings seemed to work hard both to install George W. Bush as president and to remember who it was who held the office. "Haven't seen the president yet," he gamely observed. But amid the persistent coverage of the Clintons, he [was forced] to note that they were "thronged upon arrival." There were also the verbal missteps as Jennings struggled to keep old habits in check. Al Gore was announced as "the Vice President, the Former Vice President."

At the end of the service, the rhetorical/visual tension between the rookie Bush presidency and the Clinton establishment would remain. President Bush would be whisked away, while Bill and Chelsea Clinton remained center stage, impossible to ignore. Jennings moderated the awkwardness, ratifying the Bush presidency as he worked Bill Clinton into his commentary: "The presence of Former President Clinton and of course President Bush today reminding us how important it is to the nation as a whole and always has been that the president be such a healing factor for the nation. Former President Clinton at the time of the Oklahoma City tragedy, President Bush today." But old habits die hard. As Jennings worked both to remind viewers of the absent president, and the reasons for his departure, he again misspoke: "At the risk of misjudging this **the president, the former president** gives the impression at least that he is for the moment reluctant to leave. Of one thing we are certain, the Secret Service would not have allowed President Bush to linger under current circumstances and the president in his motorcade is already on his way back to the White House. Before this day is over **the president, the current president** will be here in New York City, which is eager to welcome him." Jennings doth, perhaps, protest too much. Arguably, the need to mark someone as "the current president" can only undermine the role.

But the president who entered the cathedral was not the one who left. Everything in the intervening ceremony had already ratified both his role and his policies.

Even before the Bushes' arrival, my local network had underscored the events of September 11 and the Bush presidency. As the camera fixed on Hillary and Chelsea Clinton, subtitles read "94 CONFIRMED DEAD IN N.Y.C." and "OVER 4,700 STILL MISSING IN NEW YORK." As the scene switched to ground zero, one saw, "PRESIDENT BUSH TO VISIT NEW YORK TODAY," "VP CHENEY MOVED TO CAMP DAVID."

Amid these constructions of identity—church/state/military, former and current leaders—George W. and Laura Bush had arrived and taken their seats. The first pew facing the pulpit held, respectively, the president (on the center aisle), his spouse, his parents, then the former first family. Jennings had already noted, "The former president's wife, Senator Clinton of New York, attending in her individual right as a member of the U.S. Congress."

## A SERVICE

To understand how events built upon themselves requires a brief sequential discussion of the service. Immediately upon the Bushes' arrival, the ceremony took on a military cast, with precision marching by uniformed soldiers. As flags were carried to the front of the church, my local station provided sequential subtitles underscoring the military response to an emergency:

PRESIDENT BUSH TO CALL UP THOUSANDS OF RESERVES FOR THE FIRST TIME SINCE THE GULF WAR

CONGRESS OK'S DISASTER BUDGET, MILITARY ACTION

HELPING KIDS COPE–LOG ON TO KOMOTV.COM

LOCAL MILITARY BASES ON HIGH ALERT

SECOND ROUND OF HIJACKINGS SUSPECTED

RAIN HAMPERING NYC RESCUE EFFORTS

When the soldiers reached the front, Jennings explained the proceedings, "The presentation of the colors. The respective military services with their colors. All of those ribbons representing battles that they have participated in, in the course of the country's history." My screen continued with the toll from our current war, "200 NEW YORK FIREFIGHTERS MISSING" and "57 NEW YORK POLICE OFFICERS MISSING."

After the processional hymn, "Oh God Our Help In Ages Past," Bishop Jane Holmes Dixon welcomed the assembled. As she did so, she, too, helped install the president, then wrapped the service in his mantle. She began, "President Bush ... we want you to know that we are grateful that you called for this service and that you have brought people to this cathedral church." After words of inclusion and faith, she ended: "Thank you Mr. President and welcome to all of you to the Cathedral Church of St. Peter and Paul, the National Cathedral, and most importantly, a house of prayer for all people."

Within this site of power, emblems of inclusion were ubiquitous. The service had begun with welcoming remarks by Bishop Jane Dixon and would move to an invocation by Dean Nathan Baxter. The speakers included a Muslim imam, a Jewish rabbi, and a Catholic cardinal. As though to explain the presence of the rabbi, Jennings observed after Rabbi Haberman's reading from *Lamentations*, "The point here of course of this national presidential prayer service is to represent to the country and the world the ecumenical coming together in a time of crisis."

As Dean Baxter walked to the pulpit, Jennings provided privileged information on his perspective, "We talked to him earlier today and he said we must respond with justice, not revenge." Baxter's remarks would both ratify the nation's leadership and pose a warning.

After brief reference to Jeremiah, the Dean constructed the nation, feminine in its grief: "Today we gather to be reassured that God hears the lamenting and bitter weeping of Mother America because so many of her children are no more." Then he asked for divine wisdom for our leaders. This was, as Bishop Holmes had framed, a service of leaders, most particularly the president. But as Baxter offered a caution, he was cautious not to target the president alone. His call for wisdom was for a generic management team. In the following brief remarks, he seemed to make two moves: one was to ratify the status quo—the institution of the presidency ("our leaders"), its military action ("necessary actions for national security"), and the naming/construing of evil; the second was a veiled admonition against revenge, as Jennings had foreshadowed: "Let us also pray for divine wisdom as our leaders consider the necessary actions for national security. Wisdom of the grace of God that as we act, we not become the evil we deplore."

A brief linguistic detour is informative here. Notice that Dean Baxter could have chosen several modifiers for "necessary action": he could have used nothing, simply "necessary action," (as our leaders consider necessary action) or "*any* necessary action," as well as his choice, "*the* necessary action." What distinguishes the use of what linguists call the "definite article" (*the*) is the assumption that the item already exists, is a given: "*a* car" becomes "*the* car." By choosing the definite article, Dean Baxter arguably signals his acceptance that (presumably military) action will be necessary for national security. And that military action will be taken against those already defined as evil. Bush will take "the necessary [given and approved] actions."

In Chapter 1, "Terror or War: The War on Terrorism," we saw the building of the dichotomy between an "evil" *them* and a national *us*. The ratification of Bush's designation of "evil" would resonate throughout this service. It was used in prayers by Dean Baxter, Reverend Caldwell, Imam Dr. Siddiqi (five times), the Reverend Dr. Billy Graham (five times), and three times by commentator Jennings.

Unique among those by invited speakers, prayers by the imam and the rabbi did not reference war. Rather, they (re)constructed a peaceful America that they hoped would return. Imam Dr. Siddiqi asked for comfort and that the Lord "keep us together as people of diverse faiths, colors, and races, keep our country strong for the sake of the good and righteousness, and protect us from all evil." Rabbi Emeritus Haberman said, "As we read these lines, we as Americans reaffirm our faith and our hope that security and peace will be fully restored in our country." Perhaps because the imam's remarks also included a strong denunciation of "evil," they were posted on the United States Information Service Web site.[10]

These prayers were quickly followed by those of Reverend Kirbyjon Caldwell. His remarks echoed those of Dean Baxter: Baxter's "lamenting and bitter weeping" was paralleled by our "heavy and distraught hearts." "The evil we deplore" became "The evil hand of hate and cowardly aggression." And he, too, seemed to ratify military action in the service of national security when he asked that leaders be guided "in the momentous decisions they must make for our national security." But there were two interesting variations. First was Caldwell's explicit call for caution, not only with respect to revenge, but against racial profiling (something with which his largely African American congregation might well be familiar): "save us from blind vengeance, from random prejudice and from crippling fear." The second variation was the reference to our leaders. Unlike Baxter, who referred only to generic "leaders," Caldwell (friend of the president) also mentioned Bush by name, but in a particularly nonsecular way. He referred to the president, not by his family name, but by his "Christian" name (something he can do both as clergy and friend). In an almost biblical phrasing, Caldwell put the president on notice that he must be guided by faith: "Guide our leaders, especially George our President. Let the deep faith that he and they share guide them in the momentous decisions they must make for our national security."

Again, notice the linguistic marking of given or assumed, as opposed to new information. We don't hope that George is a man of faith. Rather, that faith is already assumed, "Let the deep faith that he and they share guide them." This can work almost as a challenge, for *if* George is a man of faith, he must be guided by it. On the national day of prayer, prayers centered not only on the healing of the nation, but on the leader of the nation.

Cardinal McCarrick read from *Matthew*, before an elderly Reverend Billy Graham[11] was helped to the pulpit. As Graham made his way, Jennings introduced him: "Dr. Billy Graham ... frail at least in body... but no man has preached the Gospel to more people in more live audiences. ... To the best of our knowledge, more than 200 million people in 185 countries have heard Dr. Graham, and the country wishes clearly to hear this man today who has been such a friend to so many presidents." Friendship with America's best-known preacher can help ratify a presidency.

Dr. Graham, too, began by thanking the president for this installation of religion into the national life: "President and Mrs. Bush, I want to say a personal word on behalf of many people. Thank you, Mr. President for calling this Day of Prayer and Remembrance. We needed it at this time." Like others, he renders the nation theistic: "we've always needed God from the very beginning of this nation." And, as had other speakers, Graham affirmed the theistic, but inclusive nature of the gathering, "We come together today to affirm our conviction that God cares for us, whatever our ethnic, religious or political background may be." Mindful of the tension we've noted between inclusion and Christianity, elsewhere he clarified, "I'm speaking as a Christian, now." Graham, too, implicitly reaffirmed support for Bush's War on Terrorism, "We're facing a new kind of enemy. We're involved in a new kind of warfare." And as had so many others, Graham began and ended with reference to the president. Toward the end of his remarks, he acknowledged the office of the president in the context of prayers for wisdom: "We also know that God is going to give wisdom and courage and strength to the President and those around him."

After mezzo-soprano Denyce Graves sang the Christian "Lord's Prayer," Dean Dixon offered a prayer for leadership. Significant here are the echoes of two themes. The first is leadership (and divine intervention on their behalf), the second remains the awkward tension between inclusion and the majority religion: "We pause now to thank you for our leaders, we pause now to thank you for all of our leaders, the seen and the unseen, the known and the unknown, those who have led in the limelight and those that have led in the shadows. Bless them and keep them and equip them to do your work. … Respecting persons of all faiths and traditions, I humbly submit this prayer in name of Jesus the Christ. Amen."

Finally it was time for George W. Bush, rhetorically now installed repeatedly as the president, to make his address to, as Jennings would refer to them later, "members of this cathedral and … the members of that congregation of the country." Now Jennings simply said, "And now the president." As the president stepped to the pulpit, Jennings expounded, "We can only imagine his burden, the country shares surely the several prayers for him and his leadership to lead the nation out of this crisis, out, one might say on this occasion, of this valley of evil." This last phrase conflates Bush's "evil" of terrorism with the "valley of the shadow of death" in the 23rd Psalm. Bush stood now under the aegis of leadership and nationalism, war and prayer.

His rhetorical task had been aptly articulated that morning in a *Christian Science Monitor* article, titled "Bush's Two Tasks; Lead, Heal Nation."[12] The article observed that "In his daunting dual role, his performance as commander so far trumps that of pastor." And it noted the possibilities the day held, "His declaration of today as a national day of prayer—and his planned visit to New York—may help assuage the country's grief." Quoting President Clinton's chief of staff, Leon Panetta, it observed, "Part of being president is being the nation's chaplain." This was the role Bush had come to the church to fulfill. (The full text of his sermon can be found in the Appendix to this chapter.)

The president spoke for seven minutes—remarks that were clearly meant to heal. We do not know how much of his speech he actually crafted. But as he spoke these words, they were his.[13] He began in the role that the *Monitor* had termed "pastor in chief," speaking both to and for the nation: "We are in the middle hour of our grief. So many have suffered so great a loss, and today we express our nation's sorrow. We come before God to pray for the missing and the dead, and for those who love them."

At several points in his speech, he returned to the pastoral role. Here is one segment:

God's signs are not always the ones we look for. We learn in tragedy that his purposes are not always our own. Yet the prayers of private suffering, whether in our homes or in this great cathedral, are known and heard, and understood.

There are prayers that help us last through the day, or endure the night. There are prayers of friends and strangers, that give us strength for the journey. And there are prayers that yield our will to a Will greater than our own.

This world He created is of moral design. Grief and tragedy and hatred are only for a time. Goodness, remembrance, and love have no end. And the Lord of life holds all who die, and all who mourn.

This was a speech framed religiously for a prayer service. But it did more. Once again, as he had on September 11 and since then, President Bush rhetorically sutured individuals into a united nation:

We express our nation's sorrow.

We offer the deepest sympathy of the nation.

Our purpose as a nation is firm.

We see our national character in rescuers working past exhaustion; in long lines of blood donors; in thousands of citizens who have asked to work and serve in any way possible.

And we have seen our national character in eloquent acts of sacrifice.

In these acts, and many others, Americans showed a deep commitment to one another, and an abiding love for our country. Today, we feel what Franklin Roosevelt called the warm courage of national unity. This is a unity of every faith, and every background.

God bless America.

This was a poetic speech. It relied on what linguist James Paul Gee[14] calls a "poetic" in contrast to a "prosaic" narrative structure. Note the powerful effect of the parallel structuring in these excerpts (the last including a scriptural quotation):

Now come **the names**, the list of casualties we are only beginning to read. **They are the names** of men and women who began their day at a desk or in an airport, busy with life. **They are the names** of people who faced death, and in their last moments called home to say, be brave, and I love you.

They are the names of passengers who defied their murderers, and prevented the murder of others on the ground. **They are the names** of men and women who wore the uniform of the United States, and died at their posts.

They are the names of rescuers, the ones whom death found running up the stairs and into the fires to help others. We will read all **these names**. We will linger over them and learn their stories, and many Americans will weep.

As we have been assured, **neither** death **nor** life, **nor** angels **nor** principalities **nor** powers, **nor** things present **nor** things to come, **nor** height **nor** depth, can separate us from God's love. **May He bless** the souls of the departed. **May He comfort** our own. And **may He always guide** our country.

There is one other consistency that runs through the speech: the theme of war. Remarks within that category became widely quoted, especially from the first excerpt below.

War has been waged against us by stealth and deceit and murder. This nation is peaceful, but fierce when stirred to anger. This conflict was begun on the time and terms of others. It will end in a way, and at an hour, of our choosing.

Our unity is a kinship of grief, and a steadfast resolve to prevail against our enemies. And this unity against terror is now extending across the world.

America is a nation full of good fortune, with so much to be grateful for. But we are not spared from suffering. In every generation, the world has produced enemies of human freedom. They have attacked America, because we are freedom's home and defender. And the commitment of our fathers is now the calling of our time.

In this last, Bush's generation became the heirs of (WW II's) "greatest generation." The war hero, George Bush, Sr.'s commitment was rendered "the calling of our time."

With the ending of Bush's speech, came the singing of the "Battle Hymn of the Republic." Written during the U.S. Civil War, the hymn became the marching song of the Northern armies. It survives today, one could argue, because it expresses a historically important strain of national consciousness, a strain that had moved through the service—the notion of divine sponsorship, that God is on our side. Recall the opening stanza:

Mine eyes have seen the glory of the coming of the Lord,
He is trampling out the vintage where the grapes of wrath are stored,
He hath loos'd the fateful lightning of His terrible swift sword,
His truth is marching on.

In this hymn, the Lord tramples the grapes that contain his wrath. God's wrath now released against their opponents, the singers identify their cause as a divine commission, not unlike Bush's charge to defeat evil. He had explained in his speech, "Our responsibility to history is already clear: to answer these attacks and rid the world of evil." Bush would place God on his side again as he announced the bombing of Afghanistan on October 7, "May God continue to bless America."

For those who watched, President Bush scored a home run. He had risen to the level of national pastor and spoken eloquently to the nation. His standing and his policies had been ratified by the religious and governmental establishment. And the religious and military nature of his call had been linked. These two last threads were underlined in the post-event commentary.

When Jennings turned to Terry Moran, "our senior White House correspondent," he gave the floor to a discussion of faith.

Jennings: We all know in the country that the president is deeply committed to his own Christian faith, and I wonder Terry, whether you believe that he will be deeply comforted by this particular service this morning.

Moran: Ah Peter there's no question about that. Many presidents, of course, have been deeply devout men. As you notice President Carter was here. President Lincoln said it was a job that had driven him to his knees every day. And that's another time of national crises. And this is a president who is not embarrassed at all about the depth of his faith. He has a very simple and straightforward, uncomplicated, and profound faith. And this service will undoubtedly comfort him. It is one of the reasons he was, we are told, involved in helping to prepare it.

Jennings went on to construct a nation within Bush's religious mold:

Jennings: ... Bear in mind this is a national day of prayer and remembrance. So as we turn, not full time by any means, to these practical means of governing, all across the country people are involved in services and vigils, of prayer and remembrance, and I think it is clear to everybody in the country, certainly anybody who has watched that service at the National Cathedral or who has participated in a small intimate vigil in the country, has a very clear understanding of how deeply ingrained in so many people at the moment is the spirit of this, the spirit of the country and in many many many many people is the spirit of their own religion or spiritual faith.

The day, however, was more than spiritual. There remained the military thread. As the screen showed the wreckage of the World Trade Center, Jennings asked Clinton advisor George Stephanopoulos for some observations on the service.

Stephanopoulos: It's hard to look at that [service] and not think about a nation and a world coming together, and that was part of the purpose of today's ceremony. But Peter what struck me about the ceremony today is that there was so much to do in it. You know, you heard the initial prayers and they were really great calls for tolerance and temperance. ... But it was also pretty clear, to me at least, as you listened to prayers and listened to the president's speech that this was also the power structure, the establishment of the country, preparing itself and the country for war. And I thought that the most striking part of the president's remarks was we have a responsibility to history, and it's clear, to answer these attacks: "War has been waged against us and we must end it in a way at an hour of our choosing." This service was about comfort, was about condolence, it was telling the country to reach out to your neighbors and take care of those who are trying to recover from this, but it was also telling the country that we have a long struggle ahead.

Moran later agreed:

> One of the purposes, as George Stephanopoulos rightly points out, of certainly the president's remarks was not only to comfort the nation in its grief, but to prepare it. It seemed to me he did so by trying to summon the martial tradition of a nation that is not by its nature very military.

## CODA

The nation may not be very military by its nature, but on that day, along with words of solace, war talk was already in the air. The day before, Mayor Giuliani had assured Bush, "Mr President we're looking forward to your visit. It will inspire us all. And we will be with you when the United States takes firm and appropriate action to those who conducted this evil."[15] As the president addressed police, firefighters and rescue workers at ground zero,[16] someone yelled "I can't hear you." Bush's response drew multiple rounds of applause:

> I can hear you. (Applause.) I can hear you. The rest of the world hears you. (Applause.) And the people who knocked these buildings down will hear all of us soon. (Applause.)

The response of the crowd was a chant: USA! USA!

As words made way for war, two "sound bites" would make the evening news around the world: "This nation is peaceful, but fierce when stirred to anger. This conflict was begun on the time and terms of others. It will end in a way, and at an hour, of our choosing." and "USA! USA!"

# Appendix

## PRESIDENT'S REMARKS AT NATIONAL DAY OF PRAYER AND REMEMBRANCE, THE NATIONAL CATHEDRAL, WASHINGTON, D.C.

September 14, 2001, 1:00 p.m. EDT

**THE PRESIDENT**  We are here in the middle hour of our grief. So many have suffered so great a loss, and today we express our nation's sorrow. We come before God to pray for the missing and the dead, and for those who love them.

On Tuesday, our country was attacked with deliberate and massive cruelty. We have seen the images of fire and ashes, and bent steel.

Now come the names, the list of casualties we are only beginning to read. They are the names of men and women who began their day at a desk or in an airport, busy with life. They are the names of people who faced death, and in their last moments called home to say, be brave, and I love you.

They are the names of passengers who defied their murderers, and prevented the murder of others on the ground. They are the names of men and women who wore the uniform of the United States, and died at their posts.

They are the names of rescuers, the ones whom death found running up the stairs and into the fires to help others. We will read all these names. We will linger over them, and learn their stories, and many Americans will weep.

To the children and parents and spouses and families and friends of the lost, we offer the deepest sympathy of the nation. And I assure you, you are not alone.

Just three days removed from these events, Americans do not yet have the distance of history. But our responsibility to history is already clear: to answer these attacks and rid the world of evil.

War has been waged against us by stealth and deceit and murder. This nation is peaceful, but fierce when stirred to anger. This conflict was begun on the timing and terms of others. It will end in a way, and at an hour, of our choosing.

Our purpose as a nation is firm. Yet our wounds as a people are recent and unhealed, and lead us to pray. In many of our prayers this week, there is a searching, and an honesty. At St. Patrick's Cathedral in New York on Tuesday, a woman said, "I prayed to God to give us a sign that He is still here." Others have prayed for the same, searching hospital to hospital, carrying pictures of those still missing.

God's signs are not always the ones we look for. We learn in tragedy that his purposes are not always our own. Yet the prayers of private suffering, whether in our homes or in this great cathedral, are known and heard, and understood.

There are prayers that help us last through the day, or endure the night. There are prayers of friends and strangers, that give us strength for the journey. And there are prayers that yield our will to a will greater than our own.

This world He created is of moral design. Grief and tragedy and hatred are only for a time. Goodness, remembrance, and love have no end. And the Lord of life holds all who die, and all who mourn.

It is said that adversity introduces us to ourselves. This is true of a nation as well. In this trial, we have been reminded, and the world has seen, that our fellow Americans are generous and kind, resourceful and brave. We see our national character in rescuers working past exhaustion; in long lines of blood donors; in thousands of citizens who have asked to work and serve in any way possible.

And we have seen our national character in eloquent acts of sacrifice. Inside the World Trade Center, one man who could have saved himself stayed until the end at the side of his quadriplegic friend. A beloved priest died giving the last rites to a firefighter. Two office workers, finding a disabled stranger, carried her down sixty-eight floors to safety. A group of men drove through the night from Dallas to Washington to bring skin grafts for burn victims.

In these acts, and in many others, Americans showed a deep commitment to one another, and an abiding love for our country. Today, we feel what Franklin Roosevelt called the warm courage of national unity. This is a unity of every faith, and every background.

It has joined together political parties in both houses of Congress. It is evident in services of prayer and candlelight vigils, and American flags, which are displayed in pride, and wave in defiance.

Our unity is a kinship of grief, and a steadfast resolve to prevail against our enemies. And this unity against terror is now extending across the world.

America is a nation full of good fortune, with so much to be grateful for. But we are not spared from suffering. In every generation, the world has produced enemies of human freedom. They have attacked America, because we are freedom's home and defender. And the commitment of our fathers is now the calling of our time.

On this national day of prayer and remembrance, we ask almighty God to watch over our nation, and grant us patience and resolve in all that is to come. We pray that He will comfort and console those who now walk in sorrow. We thank Him for each life we now must mourn, and the promise of a life to come.

As we have been assured, neither death nor life, nor angels nor principalities nor powers, nor things present nor things to come, nor height nor depth, can separate us from God's love. May He bless the souls of the departed. May He comfort our own. And may He always guide our country.

God bless America.

http://www.whitehouse.gov/news/releases/2001/09/20010914-2.html

## NOTES

1  Paul Begala, *Is Our Children Learning: The Case Against President George W. Bush*, New York: Simon & Schuster, 2000, p. 137.
2  Alan Dershowitz, *Supreme Injustice: How the High Court Hijacked Election 2000*, Oxford: Oxford University Press, 2001.
3  "One Year Ago in TIME," *Time*, December 31, 2001/January 7, 2002, p. 33.
4  Dean Nathan D. Baxter, "Welcome, Dean Baxter," *The Chimes of Trinity Cathedral*, MMI:4, Omaha, Nebraska, April 2001. Available www.brownell. edu/trinity/chimes_2001_04_welcome_dean_baxter.htm.
5  Available http://bushlibrary.tamu.edu/papers/1990/90092900.html.
6  www.cathedral.org.
7  Major Pierre l'Enfant, cited on www.cathedral.org/cathedral/discover/history.shtml.
8  Baxter, ibid.
9  Ibid.
10  His (slightly edited) remarks may be found at http://usinfo.state.gov/topical/pol/terror/01091816.htm.
11  Available http://user.chollian.net/~b1205/Billy%20Graham.htm.

12 Abraham McLaughlin, "Bush's Two Tasks: Lead, Heal Nation," *Christian Science Monitor*, September 14, 2001.

13 Available www.whitehouse.gov/news/releases/2001/09/20010914-2.html.

14 James Paul Gee, "Units in the production of narrative discourse," *Discourse Processes* 9, 1986, 391–422.

15 "President Pledges Assistance for New York in Phone Call with Pataki, Giuliani," September 13, 2001. Available at www.whitehouse.gov/news/releases/2001/09/20010913-4.html.

16 Available www.whitehouse.gov/news/releases/2001/09/20010914-9.html.

# 3

# From News to Entertainment
## Eyewitness Accounts

It's not just the story; everyone has great stories. You need to be a great storyteller.

Aaron Brown, CNN ad for *NewsNight*

In the wake of 9/11, the media were alive with survivors' tales—stories that captured horrifying events and the fortitude of those who survived them. Like all stories, these would draw on common sense ("what any reasonable person would believe or feel or do in the same circumstance"[1]), but they would also speak to what it means to be an American. Storytelling, linguist Charlotte Linde tells us, can draw people together. It can "create group membership for [the speaker] and solidarity for [a] group."[2] Stories, by their nature, locate our very personal experiences within larger cultural norms and expectations. But for the televised narratives of September 11, the larger relevance was heavily constructed by reporters and the visual frames of the news media.

This chapter examines the role of television in creating September 11 narratives and in constructing social identities. There are two assumptions at work here in the discussion of identity, one more obvious than the other. The first is that identities are neither singular nor stable; that is, people have multiple identities, including, for example, being family members, professionals, religious (non)believers, (non)citizens. And these identities are not necessarily stable. Individuals can be seen as competent professionals at one moment and lose that identity in the next. (Consider the fate of Enron executives!) The second assumption is that identities are displayed, and thereby (re)constructed through interactions with others. One is identified as, for example, a news reporter or a reasonable person or an American on the basis of displaying recognizable features of these roles. The media can aid these displays and, in fact, (re)create collective identities. Viewers can be (re)made American through the televisual displays of the nation. All of this was at play in the aftermath of the trauma that was September 11–the "Attack on America."

## TV NEWS

A brief introduction to the norms of television news coverage will be helpful here. In his analysis of news discourse, linguist Ron Scollon[3] distinguishes between the prerogatives of reporters and presenters (that is, newscasters) versus those he calls newsmakers. The former are given their authority by virtue of their role within an organizational framework. On the morning of September 11, newscaster Aaron Brown had recently assumed his organizational standing as one of CNN's principal anchors. According to *People* magazine, "Brown tailed a speeding New York City police car through red lights to his office to begin covering what he calls 'the biggest story of my life'."[4] But what was he to present?

"News," Anthony Bell tells us, "is what an authoritative source tells a journalist."[5] In contemporary coverage of major events, one often sees little of the event and a great deal of eyewitnesses and officials–Scollon's newsmakers. Newsmakers are delegated the floor (put in front of the camera) by the authority of the reporters. They may not "take the floor" on their own nor introduce their own topics. Typically, their role is to provide raw material for journalists' stories. But what happens when the material is still "raw" at airtime? The role of newsmakers is complicated in the context of the continuous, immediate, potentially unedited coverage of "Breaking News," as was the case on September 11. In such circumstances, the raw material can become the story. But we will see later that even in this "real-time" coverage, the framing by newscasters and the (tele)visual production of Breaking News manufactures a television narrative that is quite different from storytelling among friends.

A further complication for those who reported the events of September 11 is the increasing conflation of news and entertainment. Increasingly, news reports cover the emotional reactions of people (even reporters) to events, rather than the events themselves; that is, coverage is not so much about the occurrences themselves as it is narrations about them. This leads to an interesting reversal. Scollon notes that as journalists show more of their feelings, nonjournalists (eyewitnesses or "people on the street") are transformed discursively into "news-knowledgeable commentators."[6] As nonjournalists take on more of the style of the "authoritative, knowledgeable reporter," the reporters provide "entertainment" through emotion-laden commentary. Note the use of the term *entertainment* here does not imply that the content is necessarily enjoyable. This was certainly not the case on 9/11. But it contrasts with the senses of the term *news*.

Finally, Scollon notes that the primary social interaction displayed in news reporting is arguably not between reporters and viewers, but rather among journalists, as they produce a spectacle for the benefit of the viewers.

## THE NEWSCASTERS

Such were the television news conventions on 9/11 when Aaron Brown presented CNN reporter Richard Roth with one of the first eyewitness accounts of the day. Brown began with a display both of journalists' interactions and his reaction to the events. Following a report on shutting down airports and Disney World, he observes:

> Someone said to me a moment ago that before the day is over everything is going to be shut down, and that seems ta- to be where we're headed. Ah CNN's Richard Ross is on the, ah Richard Roth rather, is on the streets of New York and he can join us now. Richard, what can you tell us?

Brown enacts his institutional role by defining the situation and introducing the topic. In this instance the topic is rather broad ("What can you tell us?"), perhaps underscoring his lack of prior knowledge and the unedited immediacy of the coverage. We are watching a conversation between journalists.

With that delegation, Richard Roth (his organizational status displayed on screen: "Richard Roth/CNN New York") begins. He is literally standing on the street, and we see later what appears to be a line of people waiting for the opportunity to "report." Roth's introduction draws heavily on "entertainment." Terms that heighten emotion and intensify the description are highlighted below.

Aaron, New Yorkers think they've seen everything but ah they'll never, they'll say they- they're **amazed** at what has happened, **stunned**. Right now behind me, what **normally** would be the World Trade Center is no more. A **huge** cloud of white smoke. And right now it's **like a war zone**. Thousands of New Yorkers **streaming** north. The mayor of New York City, Rudy Giuliani, has told everyone to get north of Canal Street. We're several miles north of it. Ah right now New Yorkers are trying to get out of Manhattan. There's a ferry on the west side going to New Jersey, it's really the only access out. The mayor advising ah that people should take the subways. We have seen **dozens** of emergency vehicles, **hundreds**. Firemen being bussed in, decamp- decontamination vans coming in, calls for blood donations, for New Yorkers, their faces their expressions—**stunned, amazed** right now. With us several of those people who witnessed some of the **carnage** today.

## A NEWSMAKER NARRATIVE

With that, Roth delegates the floor to person-on-the-street, Colleen. Before turning to Colleen's narrative it is worth reiterating a caution from the Introduction to this book. To analyze the mediated linguistic constructions of these events is not to minimize their horrific nature. And some readers may prefer not to read this graphic survivor narrative. My assumption is that language plays the central role in creating human societies. If citizens are to have any role in building a post-9/11 world, we need to examine the way in which our understandings are created and manipulated through language, in particular, how events are managed and manufactured through the mass media. In that spirit, Colleen's narrative will be examined with some care. Note that I have used pseudonyms for the three survivor narrators in this chapter, those who appeared in real time (Colleen, Mr. Gonzalez, and Mike Cartwright). Colleen's is produced in response to a question from CNN's Roth:

Tell us what you saw when you exited the subway station due to a lack of smoke, Colleen

Roth's obvious misspeaking ("due to a lack of smoke") adds to the unedited immediacy as we watch Breaking News.

Um, it was very smoky and then we exited on Church Street out of the PATH train station. Um, I crossed over to Church and ah Fulton, and I was trying to get a cell phone. I was trying to get up the block, and I turned around and saw this tremendous fire. I thought it was a bomb, I couldn't see a plane. And I saw people jumping out of- off the building, many, many people just jumping. And in a panic, I had my bag and my cell phone and everything, and I was trying to find a phone because the cell phone wasn't working. Everybody was screaming, everybody was running, the cops are trying to maintain the calm. And in that haste people were stampeding. People started screaming that there was another plane coming. I didn't see the plane but I turned around and it just- the second building just exploded, and again all the debris was flying towards us. There was a woman on the ground with her baby, people were stampeding the baby. Myself and another man threw ourselves over the baby and pushed into the building. I got up and I just ran. And I ran towards towards City Hall. Then I said "oh God why am I running there?" And then I started to run towards the water. And then ah, I was by probably Spring Street, or- or- or I'm sorry Prince Street? I was at a pay phone and I heard the rumbeling [phonetic spelling]. I thought it was another bomb, I thought it was another building close to me. And then I just ah- ran from the pay phone. The man is grabbing me back telling me, "Stay here you're safe." I was like, "No way, I'm getting outta here. Go north." And then I ran into a shoe store because I wanted to call my husband, that's all I wanted to do. I wanted him to know I was alive because he knew I was in the World Trade. And um I got my office, and they connected me to my husband, and then we heard the second fall of the World Trade Center. And I- I'm astonished by the bombing. I just want to make a statement that these New York policemen and firemen, God bless them, they kept us calm, they tried so hard to keep us moving north. And it was just absolute, absolute horror, it was horror.

*And when you look back there at what would be the Nor- the World Trade Center?*

[

It's devasta-
ting, I can't look back. My six-year-old just last week asked my husband and I to take him to the [voice breaking] observation deck, and it's gone. And you know what? Americans will persevere. And I don't think that we'll stoop to the level of these zealot, terrorist pigs. And we won't kill children, I hope, and mothers. But you know what? Whatever we have to do to eradicate the country or the world of this- of this vermin, I just hope Bush will do whatever is necessary to get rid of them. And I don't know, don't know what the root of, what they, of what the answer is

[

*Al- alright thank you very much.*

We will examine Colleen's narrative from several perspectives. First is its structure as a well-formed narrative. Live television doesn't permit the luxury of leaving poor interviews on the cutting-room floor. To some extent, Colleen likely demonstrated herself to be a competent storyteller before she was allowed on camera.

Linguist William Labov argues that fully formed oral narratives have six parts:[7]

1 *Abstract:* What is this story about?
2 *Orientation:* Who, when, where, what?
3 *Complicating action:* Then what happened?
4 *Evaluation:* So, what? Why is this interesting, or how do you feel about it?
5 *Result or resolution:* What finally happened?
6 *Coda:* That's it. I've finished and am bridging back to the present.

The abstract and the coda are considered optional. Evaluations can appear throughout a narrative, at each stage explaining and evaluating events and justifying tellability. Research shows that speakers who omit an orientation or evaluation are less favorably received, as was the case for working class speakers with only a basic education in one European study.[8]

In contrast, Colleen's story is rich in orientation, detail, explanation, and evaluation. For readers who wish to examine its narrative structure in detail, it is presented in chart form in the Appendix to this chapter. Here it is worth noting that orienting statements indicating Colleen's location appear throughout her gripping narrative. Similarly, evaluative statements explaining her reasoning and feelings are also plentiful (e.g., "I was trying to get a cell phone"; "I thought it was a bomb"; "God bless them, they kept us calm").

We will see later what happens on live TV to a narrator with a less successful narrative structure. But for now we will remain with Colleen. Through her telling she establishes her identity on several fronts. Two of these work together: she is both a competent narrator and a competent person. As a narrator, she orients us more than once and evaluates the story continuously, alerting the listener to the significance of her actions.

Through her narrative construction, Colleen identifies herself as a competent person. In the midst of this crisis she has what one would need: her bag and her cell phone, and she's already discovered what everyone else in lower Manhattan will learn on that day: cell phone service was largely wiped out. People around her are "screaming," but she keeps her head. Her goals are clear: Colleen is simultaneously evaluating her decisions in terms of both her safety and her role as a responsible spouse. She must save herself and call her husband to let him know that she is safe. Colleen motivates her decisions in terms of one of these two imperatives. In fact Colleen's competence as a person is mirrored in the structure of her story, which can be understood in terms of these two complementary strands. Here is the story again. References to gaining safety have been bolded; references to reaching a telephone are underlined. Rhetorically and actually, both strands reach completion.

Um, it was very smoky and then we exited on Church Street out of the PATH train station. Um, I crossed over to Church and ah Fulton, and I was trying to get a cell phone. **I was trying to get up the block,** and I turned around and saw this tremendous fire. I thought it was a bomb, I couldn't see a plane. And I saw people jumping out of- off the building, many, many people just jumping. And in a panic, I had my bag and my cell phone and everything, and I was trying to find a phone because the cell phone wasn't working. Everybody was screaming, everybody was running, the cops are trying to maintain the calm. And in that haste people were stampeding. People started screaming that there was another plane coming. I didn't see the plane but I turned around and it just- the second building just exploded and again all the debris was flying towards us. There was a woman on the ground with her baby, people were stampeding the baby. Myself and another man threw ourselves over the baby and pushed into the building. **I got up and I just ran. And I ran towards towards City Hall. Then I said "oh God why am I running there?" And then I started to run towards the water**. And then ah, I was by probably Spring Street, or- or- or I'm sorry Prince Street? I was at a pay phone and I heard the rumbeling. I thought it was another bomb, I thought it was another building close to me. **And then I just ah- ran from the pay phone. The man is grabbing me back telling me "Stay here you're safe." I was like "No way, I'm getting outta here. Go north**." And then I ran into a shoe store because I wanted to call my husband, that's all I wanted to do, I wanted him to know I was alive because he knew I was in the World Trade. And um I got my office and they connected me to my husband, and then we heard the second fall of the World Trade Center. And I- I'm astonished by the bombing. I just want to make a statement that these New York policemen and firemen, God bless them, they kept us calm, they tried so hard to keep us moving north. And it was just absolute, absolute horror, it was horror.

Gripping as these details are, the tellability of Colleen's story does not rest on her identity as a competent person alone. Colleen's narrative builds a sense of what it means to be human, to be a New Yorker, then an American, and a citizen of the world. Recall that storytelling can be used to create group membership for oneself and solidarity for a group. Stories locate one's very personal experience within cultural norms and expectations. In Colleen's world, people do the right thing. No normal person under normal circumstances would trample a baby. Colleen tells us that *in that haste* people were stampeding. And noticing that, Colleen and another man throw themselves over the baby. This is the only complicating action that is not followed by an evaluation, an explanation. In the absence of evaluation, doing the right thing becomes the default; it establishes a particular collective identity.

Colleen's narrative moves from individual to collective identity. She has already established herself as a New Yorker. She details the local geography and refers colloquially to "the World Trade." But she also creates solidarity with other New Yorkers, who, under God, do the right thing:

> I just want to make a statement that these New York policemen and firemen, God bless them, they kept us calm, they tried so hard to keep us moving north.

Next, Colleen creates the listeners as Americans—a "we" who "persevere," don't "kill children and… mothers," and "do whatever is necessary"—this in contrast to "zealot, terrorist pigs" and "vermin" (certainly "them"). Here Colleen creates group membership for herself and solidarity for the group:

> And you know what? Americans will persevere. And I don't think that we'll stoop to the level of these zealot, terrorist pigs. And we won't kill children, I hope, and mothers. But you know what? Whatever we have to do to eradicate the country or the world of this- of this vermin…

Perhaps most significant, Colleen becomes an early media voice to rhetorically ratify George W. Bush as the commander in chief: "I just hope Bush will do whatever is necessary to get rid of them."

Colleen's presence on CNN renders her more than a storyteller. She has been delegated the role of newsmaker. Her gripping account certainly fulfills the "entertainment" imperative of contemporary news reports—again, not in the sense that these horrific images were enjoyable, but in the sense of a focus on the visual and on emotional reactions to events. Colleen is asked only two questions. The first is visual: "Tell us what you saw." The second requests an emotional reaction: "And when you look back there at what would be- used to be the World Trade Center?" In fact, this late focus on emotion elicits the only loss of composure in Colleen's lengthy description.

Throughout, however, Colleen constructs herself as another kind of newsmaker as well. Recall that Scollon argues that as journalists show more of their feelings, nonjournalists are transformed discursively into news-knowledgeable commentators. Nonjournalists take on more of the style of the authoritative, knowledgeable reporter. And Colleen takes this role seriously. Although Colleen makes a number of false starts, she makes only one apology: "And then ah, I was by probably Spring Street, or- or- or I'm sorry Prince Street." One can easily understand the need for self-correction, but the impulse to apologize is intriguing. Formal apology for slight inaccuracies would not seem to be required of her. Apologies display an expectation that one should produce a different behavior, in this case, greater accuracy. Arguably, Colleen's apology constructs her as a reporter for an audience that values accurate description of the local geography. This she provides. She begins by presenting her precise location and continues throughout to chart her course.

But, notwithstanding Colleen's journalistic instincts, she is not a newscaster; she has no institutional authority to speak. She has only been delegated the floor by a reporter who simultaneously delineates her topic: what she saw, how she feels. When Colleen begins to go beyond that, the hook takes her off the stage:

> And I don't know, don't know what the root of, what they, of what the answer is
> [
> Al- alright thank you very much.

And Roth produces a closing frame:

> A lot of other New Yorkers here continuing the evacuation of lower Manhattan. Back to you Aaron.

With that, Brown takes up the presenter role. He cohesively brackets the story with a return to the theme of shutting things down and shares his own reactions.

> Ah thank you Richard very much. Ah we told you a bit ago that the border, the U.S.–Mexican border was at a high state of alert- has

been essentially closed down, shut down. We're now told that the U.S.–Canada border is also in a high state of alert. So essentially what officials are trying to do is seal off the country. So if anyone is either trying to get in or get out, ah it's gonna be a whole lot harder to do that. Ah, but what is possible and what is imaginable I guess changes on a day like this.

Clearly, a great deal of framing work has been done both by the newscasters and the newsmaker. But, in this respect, the description thus far is only partial. Contemporary technology allows networks a great deal more visual framing.

## MANUFACTURING THE NEWS

During the course of Colleen's narrative, the screen is framed in complex ways. Throughout, the CNN logo appears in the lower right-hand corner, sometimes surmounting the word LIVE. On the left side, approximately one-third of the way from the bottom of the screen is the heading BREAKING NEWS appearing above the slogan AMERICA UNDER ATTACK. Under these appear two levels of changing headlines. One is static; in the transcript below, it is indicated in capital letters at the point that it first appears. Below that, moving headlines sometimes appear. These are indicated below in lower-case letters at the point that they first appear. Although the static heads (indicated in capitals) occasionally appear without moving titles, the reverse never occurs.

A further visual aspect of this construction is what fills the screen while we hear Colleen's voice. We begin by seeing Colleen in a small box next to a larger one that replays scenes of the World Trade Center attack and the attendant chaos. Colleen momentarily fills the screen, and then, for most of her narrative, we watch scenes occasionally labeled either "earlier" or "live." Colleen fills the screen momentarily at the end, then ends in her small box. For much of her narrative, then, we are watching current or prior footage of the event. Colleen's narrative becomes raw material after all. In the course of its telling, it is manufactured to conform to the entertainment conventions of documentaries. She becomes a "voice over."

What is the effect of these multiple layers of information on the screen? One common linguistic theory of conversation is that people attribute logic to the statements made by others even if that logic isn't obvious. For example, people work hard to make sense of a statement, even if they've misheard it. This accounts for much humor, for example, the tirade by *Saturday Night Live*'s Emily Litella (Gilda Radner), who asked, "What's all this about violins in the street?" So one might assume that the titles framing Colleen's narrative invite a kind of active sense-making on the part of the viewer, even if these titles appear at random. They certainly allow (one could argue, invite) the construction of secondary narratives. In bracketed italics below, I indicate my own parallel narrative, a construction afforded me by CNN's framing.

## MAJOR FEDERAL BUILDINGS EVALUATED IN WASHINGTON AREA

### Plane believed to be an airliner crashes into Somerset County, Pennsylvania

Someone said to me a moment ago that before the day is over everything is going to be shut down, and that seems ta- to be where we're headed. Ah CNN's Richard Ross is on the, ah Richard Roth rather, is on the streets of New York and he can join us now. Richard, what can you tell us?

*[Everything's being shut down and buildings are being evacuated.]*

### Part of Pentagon collapses after airliner reportedly crashes into military nerve center

Aaron, New Yorkers think they've seen everything but ah they'll never, they'll say they- they're amazed at what has happened, stunned. Right now behind me, what normally would be the World Trade Center is no more. A huge cloud of white smoke. And right now it's like a war zone. Thousands of New Yorkers streaming north. The mayor of New York City, Rudy Giuliani, has told everyone to get north of Canal Street. We're several miles north of it. Ah right now New Yorkers are trying to get out of Manhattan. There's a ferry on the west side going to New Jersey, it's really the only access out. The mayor advising ah that people should take the subways. We have seen dozens of emergency vehicles, hundreds.

*[Things are collapsing and crashing all around, not just in New York.]*

**RICHARD ROTH**

**CNN NEW YORK** then,

**LOS ANGELES INTL. AIRPORT CLOSED**

**White House, Departments of Justice, State evacuated: Fires at Pentagon, National Mall**

Firemen being bussed in, decamp- decontamination vans coming in, calls for blood donations, for New Yorkers, their faces their expressions—stunned, amazed right now. With us several of those people who witnessed some of the carnage today.

*[The symbols of our government are endangered, we are preparing for the worst, and everyone is stunned.]*

**LOS ANGELES INTL. AIRPORT CLOSED**

Tell us what you saw when you exited the subway station due to a lack of smoke, Colleen.

[Colleen in small box.] Um, it was very smoky and then we exited on Church Street out of the PATH train station. [Colleen in full screen.] Um, I crossed over to Church and ah Fulton,

*[Our transportation system—subways and planes—is under attack.]*

**TERROR ATTACKS AGAINST TARGETS IN NEW YORK AND WASHINGTON**

**FAA halts all domestic air travel, diverts flights to Canada; first time in history**

[Voice only] and I was trying to get a cell phone. I was trying to get up the block, and I turned around and saw this tremendous fire. I thought it was a bomb, I couldn't see a plane. And I saw people jumping out of- off the building, many, many people just jumping. And in a panic, I had my bag and my cell phone and everything, and I was trying to find a phone because the cell phone wasn't working, everybody was screaming, everybody was running,

*[This has been an attack of real terror.]*

## Lower Manhattan, United Nations evacuated; Philadelphia landmarks also emptied

the cops are trying to maintain the calm. And in that haste people were stampeding. People started screaming that there was another plane coming. I didn't see the plane but I turned around and it just- the second building just exploded, and again all the debris was flying towards us. There was a woman on the ground with her baby, people were stampeding the baby. Myself and another man threw ourselves over the baby and pushed into the building. I got up and I just ran.

*[Lower Manhattan is in chaos.]*

## All Capital Hill buildings, U.S. Supreme Court evacuated

And I ran towards towards City Hall. Then I said "oh God why am I running there?" And then I started to run towards the water. And then ah, I was by probably Spring Street, or- or- or I'm sorry Prince Street? I was at a pay phone, and I heard the rumbeling. I thought it was another bomb, I thought it was another building close to me. And then I just ah- ran from the pay phone. The man is grabbing me back

*[The city and national government buildings are in danger.]*

## BOTH U.S. BORDERS ON HIGHEST STATE OF ALERT

telling me, "Stay here you're safe." I was like, "No way, I'm getting outta here. Go north." And then I ran into a shoe store because I wanted to call my husband, that's all I wanted to do.

*[We're in a high state of alert and nothing is safe.]*

## 10,000 emergency personnel scrambled to Trade Center fires, eventual collapse

I wanted him to know I was alive because he knew I was in the World Trade. And um I got my office, and they connected me to my husband, and then we heard the second fall of the World Trade Center. And I- I'm astonished by the bombing. I just want to make a statement that these New York policemen and firemen, God bless them, they kept us calm, they tried so hard to keep us moving north.

*[She is describing the collapse of the World Trade Center as it is announced and shown on the screen.]*

## TERROR ATTACKS AGAINST TARGETS IN NEW YORK AND WASHINGTON

And it was just absolute, absolute horror, it was horror.

And when you look back there

*[New York and Washington are sights of terror and horror.]*

**More than 150,000 people visit the World Trade Center on average day**

at what would be the Nor- the World Trade Center?

It's devastating, I can't look back. My six-year-old just last week asked my husband and I to take him to the [crying] observation deck, and it's gone. And you know what? Americans will persevere. And I don't think that we'll stoop [Colleen on full screen] to the level of these zealot, terrorist pigs. [Colleen in box] And we won't kill children, I hope,

*[It may not be an average day today, but America will persevere.]*

## TWO PLANES CRASH INTO TOWERS OF WORLD TRADE CENTER

and mothers. But you know what? Whatever we have to do to eradicate the country or the world of this- of this vermin, I just hope

*[We'll get the vermin who attacked the World Trade Center.]*

**New York Police official calls scene "like war zone"**

Bush will do whatever is necessary to get rid of them. And I don't know, don't know what the root of, what they, of what the answer is

[

Al- alright

thank you very much.

*[We are at war and Bush is the commander in chief.]*

A lot of other New Yorkers here [pan to man who appears to be waiting to speak] continuing the evacuation of lower Manhattan. Back to you Aaron.

Aaron: Ah thank you Richard very much. [Aaron appears.] Ah we told you a bit ago that the border,

**AARON BROWN**

**CNN NEW YORK**

the U.S.–Mexican border was at a high state of alert- has been essentially closed down, shut down. We're now told that the U.S.–Canada border is also in a high state of alert. So essentially what officials

**All 24,000 Pentagon employees evacuated; part of building collapses in fire**

are trying to do is seal off the country. So if anyone is either trying to get in or get out, ah it's gonna be a whole lot harder to do that. Ah, but what is possible and what is imaginable I guess changes on a day like this.

*[The Pentagon has been attacked and we are sealing off the country.]*

What are we to make of this very televisual narrative construction? On the one hand, we have a first-hand account by a person who has survived a quite terrible event. But through its presence on television, it contributes to constructing a new collective identity, a new "them" and "us," and to ratifying the results of a presidential election which was, until September 11, still very much contested in many people's minds. But the further framing of the narrative does a great deal more. Following the early morning of September 11, television networks showed the attack and collapse of the World Trade Center over and over again. And if viewers weren't alarmed enough, the unending headlines (really sublines) continually escalated the level of concern. These messages along with the voices of people who were "one of us," helped transform an attack into an act of war. With the construction of "us" came the inevitable "them" in a place once very far away. But the movement toward war and the televised geography lessons are the subject of later chapters.

## A TRUNCATED NARRATIVE

By way of contrast, let's examine another interview, one that doesn't seem to go as well. Within an hour of Colleen's telling, Mr. Gonzalez, a maintenance worker at the World Trade Center was on the phone. Aaron Brown instructs him to "Tell me what happened." In Spanish-accented English, Mr. Gonzalez begins a narrative with apparently inadequate orientation and evaluation. Recall that the lack of these features in working-class narrators has been shown to earn low evaluations. In fact, Mr. Gonzalez is interrupted several times with requests for these features: an orientation ("how much time has elapsed") and an evaluation ("what did it *seem* like"). And, at a stage when these were sparse, the narrative is foreshortened. Activating his authority to delegate the floor, Brown brings the tale to an abrupt end: "Alright Mr. Gonzalez, let me stop you there."

In contrast to Colleen's transcript, the following does not document a synchronous performance, with interviewer and narrator working together to create a seamless description. Note that what is reproduced here is an excerpt. Mr. Gonzalez has seen truly horrific sights. To spare us some of those images, the transcript begins in the middle.

> *Mr. G:* I went back in and ah- When I went back in, I saw people- I heard ah people that were stuck on an elevator, on a freight elevator, because all the elevators went down. And water was going in, and they were probably getting drowned. And we got a couple of pipes, and we opened the elevator, and we got the people out. I went back up, and I saw one of the officers for the Port Authority Police. I've been working

there for twenty years, so I knew him very well. Ah my routine on the World Trade Center is to be in charge of the staircase and since there was no elevator service, I have the master key for all the, for all the ah ah ah staircase doors, so I went up with the police officer and a ah group of firemen. As we went up, there was a lot of people coming down. And while we got- it was very difficult to get up. When

Brown:  Mr. Gonzalez

G:  Ah huh

B:  Mr. Gonzalez, how much time has taken- has elapsed here ah in in this, as you recount the events. Did it seem like hours, minutes, seconds what'd it seem like?

G:  No it wasn't hours. It was

[

B:  But what'd it *seem* like?

G:  well, there was a, there was a big time, like a gap. It

[

B:  yeah

G:  was a gap of time. I won't be able to tell you if it was 15 or 20 minutes,

[

B:  okay

G:  but it was ah, it was a gap of time. We heard- while we were on the 33rd floor- I'm sorry on the 23rd floor, because we stopped there with the Fire Department, because their equipment was very heavy and they were out- they were breathing very hard. They took a break because they couldn't continue going up, so they wanted to take a break.

B:  yeah

G:  And ah, we have a person on a wheelchair that we were gonna bring down on a gurney, and a lady who was having problems with a heart attack, and um, and some other guy that was breathing hardly. We went a couple of floors up, while they were putting the person in the gurney, got up to the 39th floor, and we heard on the radio that ah the 65th floor collapsed. I heard it collapsed.

[

B:                                Alright, Mr. Gonzalez, let me
stop you there, um and let me add you're a lucky man it
seems like today. Thank you for joining us. Mike Cartwright, you were on the 64th floor, 65th floor?

Of course we can't know for certain why Mr. Gonzalez never reaches a
coda. So many features may have contributed to a foreshortening of his
tale. One can't help but wonder if his accented English contributes, as
well as the fact that he seems not to answer queries to Brown's satisfac-
tion. Perhaps the on-screen narrator waiting in the wings is judged to be
more telegenic than was Mr. Gonzalez on the phone.

## NEWS AS ENTERTAINMENT

The next narrator, Mike Cartwright, will have his own set of challenges
in matching his tale to the entertainment demands of television news.
What is particularly interesting in his interview are some of the questions. Below are excerpts from the interview that surround questions.

MC:    Ah, it was packed. I mean it was a knot- a virtual traffic jam in
       the staircase ah, up and down, I guess. Um, it was very full.
B:     People screaming?
MC:    No, actually everyone maintained calm, ah really well. I
       was really impressed with that. Ah, I think, ah, for some
       people it brought back memories of the bombing, people
       who had been there before when that happened, but ah I
       was amazed really. Ah we got into the stairway. We were
       moving down when the Fire Department group were
       coming up. They'd say, you know, "Move to the left,
       everyone move to the left," and everyone complied. A
       couple of people started crying a little bit, but you know we
       said, "We're gonna get outta here, we just gottu ah, just
       gotta focus and take it one step at a time."
B:     Was it noisy or was there screaming? Was there violence?

              [                        [
MC:                       no it was ah        no

B:      Was it eerie?

MC:     It- it was no fear- I mean it wasn't quiet. I mean people were talking in- in fact someone was laughing I kept hearing that. I thought that was strange. But ah, it- it was pretty normal. I- er- we didn't know what was going on. I mean, all we knew was something major had happened. …

MC:     The police were saying, "Don't look back, don't look back," and of course we made it about half a block, and I looked back, and I saw the other tower on fire, and I couldn't believe it and ah

B:      [Were you terrified? Were you terrified?

MC:     Ah yes we're- when we were stuck in that stairway, I mean, we stopped every now, it- it started to get nervous. But we never had any fear of the building collapse. I mean, we had no idea what was going on, ah so um, but once I got out, and it's still sinking in the real full severity of it. I mean it's just an awful- awful thing.

B:      That's true for everybody.

MC:     Yep, so.

B:      You're a lucky man.

MC:     I am lucky I ah I thank God very much.

B:      As well you might.

MC:     Thank you.

B:      Thank you very much, thank you.

Brown's "leading questions" attempt to get the speaker to focus on the entertainment aspects of the experience: feelings and emotions. He inquires whether people were screaming, if there was violence, if it was eerie, if the survivors were terrified. Not only were these not the case (was Brown disappointed that people weren't screaming?), but these were clearly not questions Mike Cartwright initially thought to address in building his informational narrative. Mike is a citizen turned reporter.

Mike is also a competent narrator. Below is the beginning of the interview. Note how skillfully he builds an orientation, even in the face of Brown's interruptions.

B:      Thank you for joining us, Mike Cartwright. You were on the 64th floor, 65th floor?

MC:     Sixty-fifth floor, yeah. That's where I work.

B:      Tell me what happened?

MC:     Well, I arrived at work early today.

B:      What do you do?

MC:     I work for the Port Authority
                                                [

B:                                              okay

MC:                                                     the Aviation Department, and ah I was just puttin' my stuff away, and all of a sudden we heard a loud crash, and ah the building started shaking. ...

Evidence that Mike's narrative is well received by his interviewer comes from the closing. We noted above that television newsmakers have the floor by virtue of the authority of newscasters, who can take it away at any point. Recall Mr. Gonzalez's abrupt ending. In typical conversational closings,[9] speakers build a closing by taking several turns before talk ceases. One speaker makes a preclosing invitation by indicating that s/he has nothing more to say. If this is ratified and confirmed by both parties, a conversation ends. It's not the case that speakers say nothing other than Okay/Okay in closings, but with each turn, they indicate that they have no new information or topics to raise. If they do discover they have new business, the conversation continues. Here's a typical closing:

A:      Okay.

B:      Okay.

A:      Nice to talk to talk to you.

B:      We'll do it again soon. Give my best to Sue.

A:      Will do.

B:      Thanks.

A:      Bye.

B:      Bye.

In the conversation/interview between Aaron Brown and Mike Cartwright, their closing follows a similar format, far different from the typical on-screen closing in which a newscaster simply announces that the conversation has ended ("Okay, thanks very much, back to you, Paul"). Perhaps because this is a real-time interview—one that meets the newscaster's approval—it is Mike who gets to the point of "passing," indicating no new topics. And, rather than closing immediately, Brown allows the full closing ritual to play out:

MC:     … and it's still sinking in the real full severity of it. I mean it's just an awful- awful thing.

B:      That's true for everybody.

MC:     Yep, so.

B:      You're a lucky man.

MC:     I am lucky I ah I thank God very much.

B:      As well you might.

MC:     Thank you.

B:      Thank you very much, thank you.

We have seen that in the unpredictable world of television interviews, the reporter on the street can encounter a range of speakers. Not all of them are as willing to participate as the narrators we've encountered thus far.

## NOT PLAYING

Television's tendency to turn tragedy into entertainment is not lost on the public, and it's not always greeted kindly, at least not by those who've just experienced trauma. Along with all the willing participants on 9/11, there were those who refused to play.

At one point early in CNN's coverage, the camera panned to a group of dust-covered survivors being led onto a bus. The camera moved in for a close-up as an off-camera interviewer (I) asked, "How did you get out?" The female interviewee (W) agreed to be a newsmaker/reporter, but drew the line at entertainment:

W:      The police officer told everybody to form a human chain. And we held on to each other, and he fl- flashed a light, and he directed everybody to building five. And we went out building five

I:      Did you see people bleeding?

After what linguists call a false start ("Oh everybody cou- see,"), W replied:

*W:*      You want blood, here's blood …

She lifted her skirt to show a wounded leg and, with a wave of her hand, dismissed the reporter.

Live television news can be unnerving for both the newscaster and the newsmaker. And while citizens, by and large, know how to play, they are not always game.

## SPINNING THE IMAGE: THE NEWS MAGAZINE

The unpredictable nature of live coverage explains why the television industry relies heavily on the highly edited news magazine format. This allows for carefully manufactured narratives, which can be cut and massaged until they are properly telegenic. At the same time, the immediacy of the interview format is maintained. Higher-status interviewees often prefer the control that this kind of coverage affords them.

Several networks featured interviews with Howard Lutnick in the early days after 9/11. Lutnick was the CEO of the world's largest bond firm, Cantor Fitzgerald, which had lost over 700 employees, including Lutnick's brother, in the World Trade Center. It was a tragically compelling story—one that news magazines were more than willing to tell repeatedly. Following is an excerpt from an interview with NBC *Dateline*'s Bob McKuen. It begins with a shot of Cantor Fitzgerald's door closing and moves to digitalized scenes of workers in computerized cubicles. McKuen's voice-over announces:

… You may not know its name, but one of those companies is called Cantor Fitzgerald. Cantor Fitzgerald dominates the bond market. Last year the firm did $50 trillion in business. But according to Chairman and CEO Howard Lutnick, what's made him most proud isn't his bottom line, but the kind of company it is.

Lutnick, now on screen, says:

> We are a family, we are the tightest group of people. We always have been a tight group of people, but you just don't know it- we did know it, but in this last couple of days, I mean, it's unbelievable.

As the camera pans debris of the World Trade Center and rescue workers, McKuen's voice is heard:

> And how long these past few days must have been for Howard Lutnick. In a catastrophe that's crushed an entire country, no one can have been hit harder than he has.

Lutnick on camera:

> We have lost every single person who was in the office. We don't know of any, not a single one person getting down from the 101st to the 105th floors where our offices were, not a single person.

As the interview continued, Lutnick's story is precisely "illustrated" by shots of the plane flying into the World Trade Center and the aftermath of the crash. This was the story of tragedy on a great scale. But it was also a story controlled and manufactured by both Lutnick and the media. From the perspective of the media, the news magazine format allowed them control and the ability to provide precise illustration of the tale. This was a far cry from the random shots that accompanied the real-time Breaking News coverage. The possibility of control served the interviewee as well. In the luxury of a sit-down interview, Lutnick was able to project an image of a fatherly CEO taking care of a family. In the course of these interviews, Lutnick promised to take care of that family. In the weeks that followed, he seemed to renege, then (in the face of mounting negative publicity) seems to have followed through. This was a survivor narrative played out elaborately in and by the media.

## THE FULLY MANUFACTURED NARRATIVE: *THIRD WATCH*

Finally, the media can fully manufacture a narrative—from the raw material of real people's experience, it can forge a composite story. This tactic was employed by the producers of TV's *Third Watch*, a series about rescue workers. It presented a show pieced together from the September 11 experiences of New York's men and women in uniform. In place of actors, the actual personnel were on camera. Multiple speakers produced a single narrative. The show began with a host explaining, "These are the people we portray on *Third Watch*, and this is the reason we portray them." Recall that the well-formed narrative begins with an *orientation* (Who, when, where, what?), moves to a *complicating action* (What happened?), and includes *evaluation* (What did you think? How did you feel?). As is evident in the brief transcript below, in the first moments of the hours-long show, composite versions of these elements had already been constructed. The names at the margins were shown on the screen, identifying the speakers.

### *Orientation + complicating action*

Officer Mike Freeman:

> Ah, on the 11th I had just finished my midnight tour so I left about ten after eight in the morning, 8:15. And it was just-normal day, you know, leave work, dry cleaners, post office that type of stuff, running a few errands. And I heard on the car radio that a small airplane had crashed into the World Trade Center.

Sgt. John Flynn:

> I was on the New Jersey Turnpike, ah, the turnpike extension coming into Jersey when my wife called me. She goes, "Have you heard the news?" And as I'm answering the phone, I'm walking over and I can see the smoke coming out of- out of the North Tower.

### *Evaluation*

Officer David Norman:

> Initially we thought that it might have been a small aircraft or one of these stunt people, like the guy that landed on the Statue of Liberty. Ah, we really didn't know what we had.

Officer Edward McQuade:

> I was totally unprepared for the magnitude of what I saw when I
> turned the news on. And I realized immediately, I said to him,
> "Look, I hate to cut you short, but," I said, "I think I'd better get
> to work."

Officer David Norman:

> I get in my car and drove a couple blocks to where I could see the
> Trade Center. And from what I saw, I could tell that it was no
> small aircraft that hit that building.

## *Next complicating action*

Sgt. John Sullivan:

> So we had somebody close the HOV lane, had them close down
> the Brooklyn Battery Tunnel except for emergency vehicles, and
> start out some additional equipment.

Officer Kenny Winger:

> Some guys just came running down. I said "Oh just jump in the
> back of the truck." I grabbed my bag, my uniforms, my gun-belt,
> got in the back of the truck. And I had everything … but my
> pants.

In its reporting of the events of September 11, television news offered a
range of formats through which the public heard from those who
survived the "Attack on America". All of these came to viewers through
the powerful tools of audio/visual programming. From the immediate
manufacturing of on-the-street survivor narratives to the production of
news magazines to the construction of composite narratives, all of the
tales provided by television were mediated accounts. They served to
provide a nation with a shared tale of September 11.

# Appendix

## COLLEEN'S NARRATIVE STRUCTURE

| | |
|---|---|
| *Abstract* | Tell us what you saw when you exited the subway station due to a lack of smoke, Colleen |
| *Orientation* | Um, it was very smoky and then we exited on Church Street out of the PATH train station. Um, I crossed over to Church and ah Fulton, and |
| *Evaluation* | I was trying to get a cell phone. I was trying to get up the block |
| *Complicating action* | and I turned around and saw this tremendous fire. |
| *Evaluation* | I thought it was a bomb, |
| *Complicating action* | I couldn't see a plane. And I saw people jumping out of- off the building, many, many people just jumping. |
| *Evaluation* | And in a panic, I had my bag and my cell phone and everything, and I was trying to find a phone because the cell phone wasn't working. |
| *Complicating action* | Everybody was screaming, everybody was running, the cops are trying to maintain the calm. |
| *Evaluation* | And in that haste |
| *Complicating action* | people were stampeding. People started screaming that there was another plane coming. I didn't see the plane but I turned around and it just- the second building just exploded, and again all the debris was flying towards us. There was a woman on the ground with her baby, people were stampeding the baby. Myself and another man threw ourselves over the baby and pushed into the building. I got up and I just ran. |
| *Orientation* | And I ran towards towards City Hall. |
| *Evaluation* | Then I said "oh God why am I running there?" |

| | |
|---|---|
| *Orientation* | And then I started to run towards the water. And then ah, I was by probably Spring Street, or- or- or I'm sorry Prince Street? I was at a pay phone |
| *Complicating action* | and I heard the rumbeling. |
| *Evaluation* | I thought it was another bomb, I thought it was another building close to me. |
| *Complicating action* | And then I just ah- ran from the pay phone. The man is grabbing me back telling me, "Stay here you're safe." I was like, "No way, I'm getting outta here. Go north." And then I ran into a shoe store |
| *Evaluation* | because I wanted to call my husband, that's all I wanted to do. I wanted him to know I was alive because he knew I was in the World Trade. |
| *Complicating action* | And um I got my office, and they connected me to my husband, and then we heard the second fall of the World Trade Center. |
| *Evaluation* | And I- I'm astonished by the bombing. I just want to make a statement that these New York policemen and firemen, God bless them, they kept us calm, they tried so hard to keep us moving north. |
| *Coda* | And it was just absolute, absolute horror, it was horror. |

# NOTES

1 Charlotte Linde, *Life Stories: The Creation of Coherence*, Oxford University Press, 1993. Linde builds on Livia Polanyi, *Telling the American Story: A Structural and Cultural Analysis of Conversational Storytelling*, Norwood, NJ: Ablex, 1985, p.194.

2 Linde, p. 114.

3 Much of the description of television news coverage in this section follows from the work of linguist Ron Scollon, though he is obviously not responsible for the ways in which I appropriate this research. See Ron Scollon, *Mediated Discourse as Social Action: A Study of News Discourse*, London: Longman, 1998.

4 Michael A. Lipton and Diane Herbst, *People*, December 3, 2001.

5 Anthony Bell, *The Language of the News Media*, Oxford: Basil Blackwell, 1991, p. 191, as cited in Scollon, p. 216.

6 Scollon, pp. 261–2.

7 William Labov, *Language in the Inner City*, Philadelphia: University of Pennsylvania Press, 1972.

8 Ruth Wodak, "The Interaction between Judge and Defendant," in Teun van Dijk (Ed.), *Handbook of Discourse Analysis (Vol. 4)*, London: Academic Press, 1985. Cited in Michael Toolan, *Narrative: A Critical Linguistic Introduction*, Routledge, 1988, pp. 254–5.

9 This discussion of closings is based on the work of Emanuel A. Schegloff and Harvey Sacks, "Opening Up Closings," *Semantica* 7: 289–327, 1973. Readers can find an abridged version in Adam Jaworski and Nikolas Coupland, *The Discourse Reader*, London: Routledge, 1999.

# 4

# New York Becomes America(n)

New York, to that tall skyline I come.
Paul Simon

"We Americans don't like our cities very much" former New York Mayor John Lindsay wrote in 1969. "In the American psychology, the city has been a basically suspect institution, reeking of the corruption of Europe, totally lacking that sense of spaciousness and innocence of the frontier and the rural landscape."[1] Whether we accept Lindsey's analysis as whole cloth, it is easily supported. American popular culture is replete with characterizations of New York as a world unto itself. Saul Sternberg's oft-cited *New Yorker* cover, "View of the World from 9th Avenue,"[2] shows a world devoid of specificity outside Manhattan. In return, nonappreciative jokes about New Yorkers' speech and ways abound throughout the rest of the country. Even New Yorkers have a love/hate relationship with their city. When there, New York is the center of the universe, but New Yorkers often take pride in losing their distinctiveness when they emigrate.

Perhaps for the first time since 1790—when it ceased being the federal capital—New York became archetypically American on 9/11. On that day New York became America. With the exception of scant coverage from the Pentagon (a military target), news coverage emanated from New York. The Twin Towers, a symbol of New York, became the symbol of "The Attack on America." The "innocent civilians" attacked as presumptive Americans were New Yorkers. The benefit concerts became simultaneously New York and American events. New York was the place to be (from). Fire and Police Department insignias (NYFD, NYPD) became ubiquitous. Chelsea Clinton wrote that she had become a New Yorker,[3] and *People* magazine showed Former President Clinton and his daughter on the streets of New York as they "met with rescue workers and comforted families."[4] I argued in the Chapter 2 that George Bush's journey to becoming a popularly accepted president included his pilgrimage to New York. This chapter explores the rhetorical construction of New York as an American city and Rudy Giuliani as "America's mayor."

## PERSON OF THE YEAR

When *Time* magazine selected Rudy Giuliani as its 2001 Person of the Year, the cover photo installed Giuliani within the New York skyline as a "Tower of Strength," metaphorically standing in for the Twin Towers. As New York became America's city, Giuliani became America's mayor, for *Time*, "Mayor of the World." What was it about Giuliani that so captured the American imagination?

In part it was his contradictions: his strength and his tenderness. If he wasn't androgynous, there were at least parts of his personality that resonated for both men and women, giving each permission to a range of emotions. When Giuliani showed his feelings, he made it clear that the thousands of men in uniform who needed to mourn could do just that. When Giuliani showed that calm and courage could replace fear, he showed how thousands of widows could go on. *People* magazine called him, "Stalwart and defiant, yet consoling and utterly human."[5]

The *New Yorker* argued, "He displayed all the right emotions, and he displayed them in just the right way. … Giuliani, during this terrible time, has truly been the city's father—strong and kind, firm and comforting"[6] (a statement which may tell us more about gendered ideologies of parenting than anything else). But to his credit, in this parental role, Giuliani had not been infantilizing. *Time* reported Giuliani's intelligence and foresight in convening meetings with the Centers for Disease Control and the FBI to learn about the threat of anthrax. "Giuliani treated the public like grown-ups, offering unvarnished information and never having to backtrack. When he told people not to panic they didn't."[7] The *New Yorker* confessed, "There is hardly a New Yorker who, at some point during the last three weeks, has not felt love—the word is not too strong—for Rudy Giuliani."[8]

## HEROES

Like George Bush, until September 11, Giuliani had become a subject of satire. His public portfolio included being a lame duck mayor, going through a publicly messy divorce, and fighting prostate cancer. But that resume was to change suddenly with the attack on the World Trade Center. Giuliani was clearly the right person for the moment. To scrutinize the rhetoric that framed his popularity is not to diminish the important and healing role he played in the wake of 9/11. Rather, to explore the rhetoric that propelled him to unprecedented approval ratings is to understand a great deal about the common-sense, naturalized notions of heroism that Giuliani was able to harness. He was a living hero among so many fallen.

The words used most often to describe Giuliani, along with the uniformed public servants who perished in the World Trade Center, and the passengers on Flight 93, were *courage* and *bravery*. Late-night TV host David Letterman called Giuliani, "The personification of courage."[9] More importantly, Giuliani talked about dealing with fear. Speaking about his kids, he said he tried "to help them figure out how to deal with fear. How to live life, even though you are afraid."[10] Speaking of his own fear, he said, "Courage is being afraid but then doing what you have to do anyway."[11] Courage became action in the context of duty.

It's not surprising that at a time of palpable fear, Giuliani's steadiness would be coded as courage and his demeanor glossed as a primer on dealing with fear. An interesting aspect is the extent to which these were discussed in terms of doing his job. He was described as "the indomitable mayor" and chosen to be Person of the Year, "for not sleeping and not quitting and not shrinking from the pain all around him."[12]

It is these combined characteristics—courage (in the line of) duty—that would bind the story of Giuliani to those of firefighters, police officers, and rescue workers. At the benefit Concert for New York on October 20, New York Governor George Pataki defined a "true hero"—ordinary people doing extraordinary things because these were called for:

> Time and again have we seen … courage in ordinary citizens doing extraordinary things to protect us. In these uncertain times we don't have to look any further than to these heroes for us to draw strength. We look to our firefighters, our police officers, our emer-

gency service workers who risk their lives, God bless you. We are proud of you. You are true heroes. And we are inspired by your courage.[13]

The Concert for New York honored the more than 5,000 emergency workers, firefighters, and police officers who'd been invited to attend. Giuliani—who had continuously praised the courage of people doing their jobs—spoke about the uniformed services:

> We all have a renewed appreciation for the **courage** of our men and women in uniform. We've always known this, right? What's the best fire department in the world, right? Now the whole world knows it. What's the best police department in the world? Thanks to our fire department, the police department, the Port Authority police officers, our EMS workers, our court officers, our emergency managers, together they saved more than 25,000 lives at the World Trade Center. They met the worst attack on America with the very, very best of humanity. As we face the future, we need to **take courage**, we need to continue to **be inspired** by their example.[14]

To probe the notion of courage very far is to find its opposite: cowardice. The rhetoric surrounding the attacks on New York would align America with the former term. A populace under attack was assured of its strength and bravery. The counterpoint was to rhetorically strip the terrorists of any vestige of courage. "Cowardly acts" was how President Bush characterized the attacks on September 11. Other epithets would be more obscene and feminizing, while the Americans who lost their lives became models of courage.

Another intriguing dichotomy emerged between heroes and victims. There were, of course, the "innocent victims" of September 11 and their families. But there was a stalwart resistance to feeling victimized. Over and over again, families of employees lost in the World Trade Center reported that their loved ones would have died characteristically helping others. Sting dedicated his performance at a benefit concert to a "kind, generous man who I would imagine died in much the same way as he lived his life: heroically helping other people."[15] These many tales of presumed heroism may not tell us about the fallen, but they tell us a great

deal about the living. There is, by these construals, more than one definition of *courage* and *heroism* abroad. Courage is not merely fighting others,
it is fighting for others. Acts of nonviolent selflessness became a central
element of a discourse of courage after September 11. (Discourses of
retaliation are within the purview of previous chapters.)

By October 20, and the New York Concert, Governor Pataki was able
to position a broad range of courageous heroes—all fulfilling their duty—
who could serve as inspiration for the continued strength of a populace
under pressure:

> And we're inspired by the **courage** of others, people like the passen-
> gers on Flight 93, who risked their lives and gave their lives to
> protect innocent people on the ground. We look to the **courage** of
> our children, the brave schoolchildren in lower Manhattan who
> saw horror before their eyes and nine days later went back into
> their classrooms with **incredible courage and resolve** to continue
> their education. And we look to the **quiet heroes** of this crisis. The
> fathers and mothers, the husbands and wives, the sons and daugh-
> ters of those who have lost their loved ones, the innocent victims.
> We are **inspired with their strength**, with their faith and the
> **courage** they have shown so that we will not just go on, we will go
> on to bigger and better things for New York and for America. And
> so tonight as we pay tribute to these heroes who died. Let us
> continue to show them that they have strengthened us and united
> us as a nation like never before. Their **courage** made us proud. Let
> our strength make them proud.

This focus on heroes was not without costs. In the same issue of *Time*
magazine that carried the Person of the Year, was a story about an
unwilling hero. On September 11, a photo was taken of a firefighter
rushing up the stairs in Tower One as civilians descended the crowded
stairwell. Upon its publication, the reluctant hero was deluged with
attention, something difficult for him to deal with. And the sudden
celebrity was not well received by his fellow firefighters, who resented
that he'd received more notice than their fallen brothers. *Time* aptly
described the role of the photo: "The photograph fast became part of
the redemptive fairy tale spun by Americans to make some rough sense

of Sept. 11. The good guys … saved the day, the evil ones were blotted out."

The firefighter was, by the rhetoric of the day, a hero. He had, indeed, done his job. He'd run up almost 30 flights of stairs carrying more than 100 lbs of gear, without any thought but duty—in his case to lay hose that could douse the flames. Near the 28th floor, he'd received the order to evacuate. What has been difficult for him is the disjuncture between his own sense of things—doing his job, mourning lost colleagues, feeling guilty that he is glad to have survived—and the discourse that has been created around him: "Everyone wants to know how many people the superhero pulled from the towers. The answer never changes: 'I saved one person that day, and that was me, and it was by running for my life'."[16] He is caught between his own needs—to assimilate, then move past, the events of 9/11—and the needs of a rhetoric that requires personal appearances by real-life heroes to inspire citizens and children in the wake of great loss—loss of life and of innocence.

Notwithstanding the psychological toll of tales based on reluctant heroes, the pressure to sustain them can be enormous. Narratives of survival and redemption reject the mantle of victimization and vulnerability. New York's men and women in uniform became, in the words of John Lennon, "working class heroes."

On September 20, a benefit concert coupled the mystique of New York with that of John Lennon. "Come Together: A Night for John Lennon" was dedicated to nonviolence and the people of New York. Host Kevin Spacey talked openly of social class, something that is fairly unusual in U.S. discourse:

> In his life John Lennon struggled to remain a man of the people, "a working class hero" to borrow a phrase of his own. Today we are at long last appreciating our own working class heroes. Our city's everyday protectors who so valiantly attempted to protect the lives of others and in so doing sacrificed their own. So tonight and forever let there be no doubt, a working class hero is something to be.

On October 20, in The Concert for New York, Mick Jagger echoed those sentiments as he sang for rescue workers who had endured six weeks of back-breaking work at ground zero, "Let's drink to the hard-working people."

This sense of everyday heroes was a fundamental part of the post-9/11 rebuilding. During that period, as Giuliani searched for what to say, he took his inspiration from Winston Churchill:

> It seemed to me they needed to hear from my heart where I thought we were going. I was trying to think, Where can I go for some comparison to this, some lessons about how to handle it? So I started thinking about Churchill, started thinking that we're going to have to rebuild the spirit of the city, and what better example than Churchill and the people of London during the Blitz of 1940, who had to keep up their spirit during this sustained bombing? It was a comforting thought.[17]

Churchill biographer Roy Jenkins confirms that this was an apt approach: "What Giuliani succeeded in doing is what Churchill succeeded in doing in the dreadful summer of 1940: he managed to create an illusion that we were bound to win."[18] The *Washington Post* dubbed him, "Churchill in a baseball cap."[19] Rudy Giuliani, son of Brooklyn and "a family of firefighters, cops, and criminals,"[20] had, in doing his job, become a working class hero. In so doing, he had become the embodiment of New York, and "a global symbol of healing and defiance."[21]

## NEW YORK

Rudy Giuliani's public statements reinforced the mystique of New York, something New Yorkers appreciated:

> In cheering Rudy we have also been cheering our city, and our firefighters and our cops and our rescue workers. And we have been cheering ourselves, or a familiar idealization of ourselves: the indomitable city dweller, the tough guy with a heart of gold. Giuliani became the medium for the inchoate feelings of pride and defiance and solidarity that swept over us all.[22]

On September 13, when he was told that additional rescues were extremely unlikely, Giuliani is reported to have said, "These are New

Yorkers. Give them another week."[23] Giuliani reminded New Yorkers that "what could have destroyed us made us stronger."[24]

Issues of identity and loyalty were widely discussed, and being a New Yorker by choice was valorized. Here are a few testimonials by actors from the benefit concerts for New York:

> I'm now a proud New Yorker. I live here, and John Lennon, who was also born in my parents' hometown of Liverpool, England, also chose to live in New York City. (Mike Myers)

> My husband Chad and I moved to New York in December. On September 11 in our hearts we feel like we're official New Yorkers. We're staying. (Hillary Swank)

> This evening is now dedicated to New York City and its magnificant people. … Although John Lennon was a Liverpudlian by birth, he was a New Yorker by choice. John Lennon loved New York, and New York loved and loves John Lennon. (Kevin Spacey)

Howard Stern excoriated people for leaving New York, "I just want to say something to all the celebrities who have stayed away from New York. I say shame on you. Come back to New York. Don't run, don't hide."[25] Rudy Giuliani was less accusatory in expressing a similar sentiment, "Anybody who stays away from this place is absolutely crazy. This is the greatest city in the world."

New York's sense of itself returned. The transition from shock to bluster can be seen comparing the first televised benefit concert, on September 21, with The Concert for New York on October 20. In the shocked aftermath of September 11, "America: A Tribute to Heroes" was a somber and decorous event. In New York, Los Angeles, and London, musicians performed on stark, empty stages; in the U.S. venues, hundreds of lighted candles provided a backdrop. And while it had much to say about and to New York, its narrative began by forefronting civilian heroes, from across the nation. Tom Hanks began:

> "We're gonna try and do something." That was the message sent from some very American heroes with names like Sandra Bradshaw, Jeremy Glick, Mark Bingham, Todd Beamer, and

Thomas Bennett. They found themselves aboard the hijacked Flight 93 that went down in Somerset County, Pennsylvania, on September 11, 2001. They witnessed the brutality on board and somehow summoned the strength to warn us and take action. United they stood and likely saved our world of an even darker day of perhaps even more unthinkable horror.

Hanks had followed a haunting acoustic performance by Bruce Springsteen—an iconic link between working class urban culture and the rest of America. Backed by vocalists including members of his E-Street Band, Bruce sang for New York a song he had written originally for Asbury Park, New Jersey. He sang poignantly of loss and rebuilding in "My City of Ruins," urging the city to "Come on rise up."

In contrast, there was nothing decorous about Madison Square Garden's Concert for New York. It was a raucous event, celebrating New York's uniformed personnel, designed to be a first moment to kick back after six weeks of grief and gruesome work. Former President Clinton glossed the occasion: "So many of you tonight for the first time got to clap your hands, and stomp your feet, and make a joyful noise for the first time in over a month. God bless you for doing it tonight."[26]

In place of decorum, this concert fed an irreverent self-conception. In a fake Italian accent, "Operaman" (Adam Sandler) captured the many sides of Giuliani and referred mischievously to Giuliani's early campaigns to rid New York's streets of prostitutes, drug dealers, and panhandlers:

Giuliani! Giuliani!
How we'll-ah miss you
Senior Rudy
So tough but oh so sweet
Only good thing
About-ah your leaving
We get the hookers back on the street

The Rolling Stones' Keith Richards told the rowdy crowd, "You know I got a feeling this town gonna make it," then added, "You know there's one thing to be learned from this whole experience. You don't f–k with New York, okay?" (tough guy with a heart of gold?). In the course of the evening, New York became synonymous with profanity. Introducing a film by Kevin Smith, Mike Meyers explains:

> Kevin Smith is living proof that anyone with drive, talent and heart can become a New Yorker. ... The characters of Kevin Smith's films ... exemplif[y] that one quality that identifies a true New Yorker—the ability to curse like a mother f—er.

And curse they did. Perhaps the most often cited moment came from firefighter Mike Moran:

> On behalf of my brother John and the 12 members of Ladder 3 that we've lost, the 20 members of the New York City Fire Department football team that we've lost, and all the people from my neighborhood, my home town, Rockaway Beach, Queens, New York, our friends, our neighbors, our relatives: They are not gone because they are not forgotten. And I want to say one more thing. In the spirit of the Irish people, Osama bin Laden you can kiss my royal Irish ass. And I live in Rockaway and this is my face, b-t-h. [Chanting: USA! USA! USA!]

That single piece of language became an empty vessel, which received plenty of fluid from the left and the right. Many loved it. Doug Cogan and Christopher Storc's "The Ballad of Mike Moran"[27] gained radio play, and CDs are sold on the Web. It began:

> I am Irish and was proud to serve with other firemen
> Who gave their lives for us that day, each one of them a friend
> In remembrance of my brothers who from earthly bonds did pass,
> Osama, step right up and kiss my royal Irish ass.

The firemansong.com Web site includes a message board. This posting was made in early December from Dayton, Ohio:

> Finally having read all the words to this song, I am very proud of Mike Moran and all of the firemen FDNY. Many thanks to the authors of this song, Doug and Chris, who have brought out the

pride in my Irish heart and told that ignorant lout in Afghanistan
exactly what my Irish father used to say "Kiss my royal Irish ass"!!
I am glad to hear the melody used as it was learned by me as a
child—first as "The Orange and the Green" and as I got older and
learned of the Rebellion, I learned it again as "By The Rising Of
The Moon". Very good for stirring up our Irish Blood!!
Keep up the good work, lads!!

But the "fighting words" and the concert in general also fueled debates
about class, race, and political correctness. Jim DeRogatis, a pop music
critic for the *Chicago Sun-Times*, wrote on the Web site *salon.com*, "It would
have been hard to find a rowdier, drunker or whiter group anywhere on
television, outside of a monster-truck or pro-wrestling match. ... And it
was certainly easy to dislike those heroic cops and firemen as they bum-
rushed the stage to pay tribute to fallen comrades without once
mentioning the thousands of dead office workers at the World Trade
Center."[28] Joan Walsh, editor of *Salon News*, wrote an article in response,
"Salt of the Earth: New York's Finest Got the Party They Deserved on
Saturday Night—and If You Don't Think so, You Know What You Can
Kiss."[29] Walsh takes to task the discourses of the left and the right in her
(liberal) defense of the party:

> Paul McCartney [and others] threw a party to help the grieving get
> on with their lives, to remember the dead and celebrate them too, to
> say it's OK to live. And they did a great job. ... The events of Sept.
> 11 have been hard for the simple-minded on the right and the left,
> who want their heroes perfect, their villains all-evil, their causes
> easy to understand. Who do you think died trying to save the
> World Trade Center victims that morning ... they were working-
> class guys, a vast number of them Irish and Italian, from Queens
> and Brooklyn and Long Island. Some of them drink too much and
> vote Republican. ... They deserve our unqualified gratitude. They
> deserved a big, sentimental, over-the-top party without any
> preaching, and they mostly got it. ... They're also my family. ...
> [I've learned to] respect their values, their work ethic, their tribal
> loyalty and their love—for their families, their neighborhoods, their
> brothers (and sisters) at police stations and firehouses, and their

country. ... One of my favorite cousins ... followed his father into the NYPD. I still don't like all of his attitudes about race and politics. But ... he's colorblind when it comes to his brothers. So I loved Saturday's concert for helping us remember exactly who died saving lives at the World Trade Center.

The conservative *New York Observer* exploited Moran's epithet as an opportunity to argue against civil rights. For the *Observer*'s Jim Sleeper, apparently the answer to the Taliban is our own form of racial and sexual exclusion:

Mr. Moran's manifesto offered an answer some don't want to hear: Most of the uniformed public servants who gave their lives were bound into a brotherhood that affronts civil-rights activists. At least 80 percent of New York's firefighters are white, Roman Catholic men like Mr. Moran, members of an intergenerational, "father–son" union often condemned as racially and sexually exclusive. ... Take multiculturalism ... –as Mr. Moran did, after a fashion. Some firefighters do believe that their blood-thick ties couldn't be sustained without the racial, ethnic and sexual solidarity that fired Mr. Moran's manifesto. ... And so, for better or worse, the sacrifices of old-boy networks like the one that bound Michael Moran to his lost blood brother and his brotherhood in Ladder 3 remain America's strongest answer to the Taliban's declaration that their people love death as we love life. We have shown them that we do love life, enough to risk death to save it. But the reasons run deeper than either social activists or corporate managers think.

From Mr. DeRogatis came the discourse of the cynic; Ms. Walsh's piece romanticized; Mr. Sleeper provided the rhetoric of the right, arguing that loyalty cannot survive diversity. New York had finally returned to some sense of complexity. But it had already become "America's city." New York and America were bound together in a love for Giuliani and his vision of New Yorkers as America's heroes.

Michael J. Fox introduced the mayor towards the end of The Concert for New York:

I love this city, I love the USA. But if it's possible for someone who may love this city even more than we do, for the past six weeks he's given new meaning to the expression grace under pressure. And now I hear the Queen of England is thinking of making him a knight. Through this ordeal he led with strength, clarity, and immeasurable compassion. Wherever his journey may lead, I can tell you this. His devotion to the city will never be forgotten here— tomorrow, six weeks from now, years from tomorrow, and long after that. From the bottom of our hearts we thank him. Please join me in welcoming the mayor of New York City.

By this time the audience was on its feet, a large American flag was being carried through the hall, and the audience was chanting "Rudy! Rudy!"

In his remarks, Giuliani addressed the child of a lost firefighter, as he had so many times during the preceding six weeks: "Your father, Shawn, your father is a hero and a patriot that all America respects."

## AMERICA

As New York became America's City, Giuliani became a national leader. *Time* reported that:

With the President out of sight for the most of that day, Giuliani became the voice of America. Every time he spoke, millions of people felt a little better. His words were full of grief and iron, inspiring New York to inspire the nation. "Tomorrow New York is going to be here," he said. "And we're going to rebuild, and we're going to be stronger than we were before … I want the people of New York to be an example for the rest of the country, and the rest of the world, that terrorism can't stop us."[30]

Later he said, "What could have destroyed us made us stronger." Thanks to the heroes "who turned the worst attack on American soil into the most successful rescue operation in American history."[31] After a visit to New York, Essayist Richard Rodriguez observed that "Mayor Giuliani has played a convincing Uncle Sam."[32] *Time* saw him as a "global symbol of healing and defiance."[33] *People* magazine underscored Giuliani's role in restoring hope to the nation:

> Long a larger-than-life figure ... Giuliani ... has emerged as a symbol of strength and hope for New York and, indeed, the nation. Stalwart and defiant yet consoling and utterly human, Giuliani has at once orchestrated massive relief efforts, comforted a terrified citizenry and re-established a sense of order and even optimism.[34]

Giuliani led through his dual rhetorics of strength and compassion: "Giuliani has served as fearless leader and comforting shoulder for America."[35]

The citizenry had already conjoined New York's security with that of the nation. A law firm executive with offices across the street from the World Trade Center observed, "it looks like something you'd see in the Third World. It didn't seem like New York, American at all."[36] In the midst of that destruction, *Time* argued that Giuliani had become America's homeland security chief as well as "the solemn tour guide at a mass grave, escorting the leaders of the world around ground zero."[37]

Giuliani did seem to take on a symbolic role beyond the nation. In anointing him Person of the Year, *Time* explained, "Giuliani has vaulted into the ranks of world leaders. He ignites adulation in the streets of Jerusalem. His Blackberry pager pulls in an e-mail message from the Queen of England, who is available in February to knight him."

Giuliani's celebrity helped New York play a new role. Perhaps for the first time, New York became the vehicle through which to promote a discourse of renewed unity. Giuliani affirmed at The Concert for New York, "Since the attacks of September 11, New Yorkers and Americans have united as never before." Notice the syntactic ambiguity here. Are New Yorkers united as never before—as are Americans—or are New Yorkers and Americans united together in common cause? This is the ambiguity with which New York has always lived as it has struggled to learn the world beyond 9th Avenue. But on that evening, both meanings obtained, as Giuliani continued: "We've all renewed appreciation for the blessings of freedom." Speaking of New York's men and women in uniform, he placed them within the national context and beyond, "They met the worst attack on America with the very very best of humanity."

Billy Graham, speaking at the National Cathedral on September 14,[38] had already embraced New York as part of the fabric of America:

What an example New York and Washington have been to the world these past few days! None of us will ever forget the pictures of our courageous firefighters and police, many of whom have lost friends and colleagues, or the hundreds of people attending or standing patiently in line to donate blood. A tragedy like this could have torn our country apart, but instead it has united us and we have become a **family**.

The Tribute to Heroes had echoed a similar sentiment: "We are here tonight as a simple show of unity to honor the real heroes and to do whatever we can to ensure that all their families are supported by our larger **American family**. This is a moment to pause and reflect, to heal and to rededicate ourselves to the **American spirit of one nation indivisible**."[39]

Paralleling a TV ad for America that will be explored in the next chapter, The Concert for New York aired an ad for New York. Initially, geographically and ethnically diverse Americans stated their names and where they were from: I'm from York, Pennsylvania; Boston; Rhode Island; Denver, Colorado; Fort Lauderdale, Florida; Austin; Seattle; Columbus. Then these geographical identities merged into other identities: police officer, mother, firefighter, teacher, and then, "New Yorker." The ad ended with everyone now reframed in a unity around New York: I'm a New Yorker, I'm a New Yorker, I'm a New Yorker, I'm a New Yorker.

At least for a moment, the nation's symbolic unity came through New York—a sentiment reflected in the introduction given a filmmaker in The Concert for New York: "He's like so many Americans today, a New Yorker in his heart."

## NOTES

1  John V. Lindsay, *The City*, New York: Norton, 1969, p. 50.
2  *New Yorker*, March 29, 1976.
3  Chelsea Clinton, "Before and After," *Talk*, December 2001/January 2002, p. 103.
4  "Stellar Effort," *People*, October 1, 2001.
5  "Tower of Strength," *People*, October 1, 2001.
6  Hendrik Hertzberg, "Rudy's Rules," *The New Yorker*, April 20, 2002.

7 Eric Pooley, "Mayor of the World," *Time*, December 31, 2001/January 7, 2002.

8 Hertzberg.

9 "Tower."

10 Pooley.

11 Ibid.

12 Ibid.

13 Governor George Pataki, *The Concert for New York City*, October 20, 2001.

14 Rudy Giuliani, ibid.

15 Sting, ibid.

16 Jodie Morse, "Glory in the Glare," *Time*, December 31, 2001/January 7, 2002.

17 Pooley.

18 Ibid.

19 "Tower ."

20 Pooley, ibid.

21 Ibid.

22 Hertzberg.

23 Pooley.

24 Ibid.

25 Howard Stern, *The Concert for New York*, October 20, 2001.

26 Bill Clinton, ibid.

27 Cogan, Doug and Christopher Storc, "The Ballad of Mike Moran" (www.firemansong.com/The_fireman_song.html).

28 Jim DeRogatis, "Stop this benefit!" October, 21, 2001. Available www.salon.com.

29 Joan Walsh, "Salt of the Earth," October 23, 2001. Available www.salon.com.

30 Pooley.

31 Ibid.

32 Richard Rodriguez, "Essayist Richard Rodriguez of the Pacific News Service Revisits New York City," *NewsHour with Jim Lehrer,"* December 14, 2001.

33 Pooley.

34 "Tower."

35 Pooley.

36 "Hell on Earth," *People*, September 24, 2001.

37 Pooley.

38 A slightly edited version appears at http://user.chollian.net/~b1205/Billy%20Graham.htm.

39 Tom Hanks, *A Tribute to Heroes*, September 21, 2001.

# 5

# Selling America

Make Alan Greenspan proud, buy something.
Dallas billboard selling classified ads

The Ad Council of America was founded as the War Advertising Council in 1942, in the wake of the attack on Pearl Harbor.[1] It is the group that has brought America some of its most powerful slogans, from the World War II "Loose Lips Sink Ships"[2] to Smokey the Bear's "Only You Can Prevent Forest Fires," to "Friends Don't Let Friends Drive Drunk."[3] The council is a private, nonprofit agency whose mission remains today as it was articulated in 1942:

> To identify a select number of significant public issues and to stimulate action on those issues through communications programs which make a measurable difference in society.[4]

After the attacks of 9/11, the Ad Council undertook to provide messages of tolerance and patriotism. But the council's multicultural inclusiveness was not the only advertising message on the airwaves. Two kinds of campaigns "sold America." The Ad Council's was a manifestation of nation building as it sold America on itself. The second campaign sold America on consumerism. Both promotions turned on patriotism. One built loyalty to values of tolerance and diversity. The other conflated patriotism and consumerism in a dance of political/economic codependence, resisted (at least initially) by many. The trajectory of these promotional campaigns—from tolerance to spending—is the focus of this chapter.

## AMERICA RESPONDS TO THE CRISIS

In the aftermath of September 11, the Ad Council developed an extensive media campaign titled, "America Responds to the Crisis: Messages That Can Help and Heal." President and CEO Peggy Conlon described the council's role and stance:

> The Ad Council's expertise lies in working with volunteer advertising agencies to develop social messages on behalf of our not-for-profit and government partners, and to distribute these messages to the media community across the United States. At this time of crisis, the Ad Council has assumed the responsibility to distribute the most critical messages to all Americans. Many of the ads that are currently being distributed **are not Ad Council PSAs** [public service announcements; bold in original], but have been developed by some of our country's most respected non-profit organizations, and are extremely relevant to the events we are facing.
>
> In the face of this tragedy, we at the Ad Council are gratified that we can use our expertise and resources to reach out to the American people. We are extremely grateful to the media for generously supporting our messages for nearly sixty years and are confident that you will support these as well. Thank you for your continued faith. God Bless You and God Bless America.[5]

In its government partnerships and access to the American people, the Ad Council is as close as the U.S. comes to having a national propaganda organ; it is responsible for many of the public service announcements Americans encounter on television and radio, in print, and now on the Internet. The messages of the "Crisis" campaign stressed the civic virtues of tolerance and social responsibility. But what can be seen by many as ideologically neutral public service announcements can be read quite differently by others, depending on the worldview they bring to the task.

Like all texts, these ads allowed for a range of readings, as recipients were able to project their own perspectives onto them. A few preliminary examples below will quickly underscore the complex task facing the Ad

Council as it launched its most famous PSA, "I am an American." This potential for diverse readings can be seen first in brief examples from the Web. Ad Council Internet campaigns urge Web masters to add council banners to their sites. Examples include two reproduced below. While on the screen, each line flashes, then is replaced, in a continual loop, by the next.

Whatever race
Whatever country
Whatever religion
All families worry about the same thing

Talk to your children about terrorism
Talk to your children about tolerance

Turning to the last message first, we see that these very abbreviated banners require a great deal of "filling in." This is an ad campaign that asks viewers to supply familiar cultural themes and common-sense reactions to potent terms. What is the connection between talking about terrorism and talking about tolerance? Is it causal? If so, in which direction? To demonstrate the multiple possibilities, here are a few possible interpretations, together with a pair of contrasting glosses for the banner. Readers will no doubt be able to generate many others.

- *Terrorism is caused by a lack of tolerance. Inoculate your children against terrorism; teach tolerance.* As a native speaker of "Americanese," I rather think that this is at least close to an intended, first-order message. But other possibilities abound.
- *Terrorism is caused by a lack of tolerance. If we don't teach tolerance we would become vulnerable to recruitment by terrorists.* This meaning is slightly different from the first, but plausible. It works particularly if one enters the loop seeing *tolerance* first, then *terrorism*.

Here are quite different possibilities:

- *Tolerance is a liberal term that doesn't address the underlying roots of terrorism. Explain to your children why people turn to terrorism when despair overtakes hope.*

- *Tolerance is a liberal term that doesn't address the underlying roots of terrorism. It asks the victim to embrace tolerance while being savaged. Talk to your children about the necessity of terrorism now that despair has overtaken hope.*

Finally, here are two alternative glosses:

- *This is a message that Americans write to assume moral superiority over the world's desperate and poor.*
- *This is the kind of message that would save the world if everyone could see it and be schooled in it.*

As we can see, ad campaigns cannot guarantee a single response from a diverse audience. There is presumably an infinite number of "readings" of, and reactions to, this banner. The job of advertisers is to position targeted readers as closely as possible to at least a range of desired reactions. Those sympathetic to terrorism were presumably not the targeted audience. Predicting viewer response is a challenge, but it is also the special task of advertising. A similar set of readings could arise from the first banner:

Whatever race
Whatever country
Whatever religion
All families worry about the same thing

The most obvious reading in the U.S. is the universalist one: *Don't lose sight of the commonalities of being human.* But this is not the only reaction. There is also the racist one: *This sentiment is the luxury of those who are relatively safe; "those people" don't care about their families or they wouldn't send them off to kill us and die.* And there is the reading of the desperate: *We don't have the luxury of worrying about the physical safety of a single person; we are fighting for the survival of our people or homeland or culture.*

The common-sense civic virtues that the Ad Council propounds will not resonate universally. But they do appeal to a range of readers in the U.S. Within the complex and contradictory rhetoric of the nation, these ads draw on an internal discourse of what is considered the best of America. They sell the nation to itself. They remind America of its multicultural identity at a time when that could be threatened.

One of the print ads was particularly powerful. On the skyline of New York, where the Twin Towers had been, two long columns read as follows:

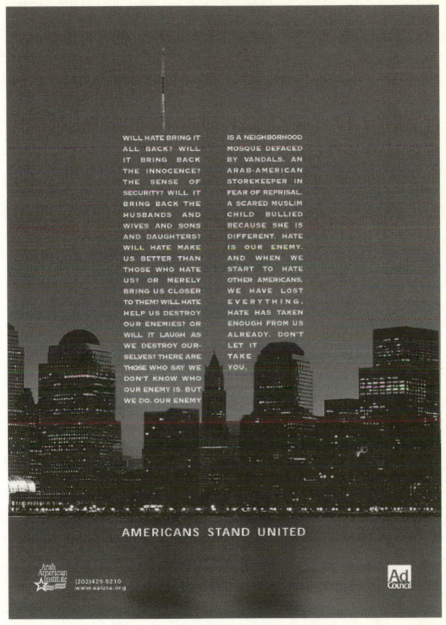

Reproduced courtesy of the Arab American Institute and the Ad Council

The ad identifies an enemy worse than the terrorists of 9/11, that is, the scourge of hate. But what does the slogan, "Americans Stand United" mean? On the one hand, it means that Americans are united against an internal enemy, in this case, hate. On the other hand, calls to stand united are a fairly standard wartime exhortation, and the U.S. was at war. Another possible reading of the full ad focuses on an external enemy: America will not be able to fully unite in the War on Terrorism if it is internally fractured by divisive hate. And at a distance, the ad scans like typical patriotism, urging unity in support of the current war. This combination of themes, inclusion, unity and traditional patriotism (along with the diverse readings they allow), became the Ad Council signature in several ads.

Inclusion and unity are joined in two additional PSAs reproduced opposite and on page 114. Like other ads, these came with admonitions against division in a time of national crisis. "We all came over in different ships, but we're in the same boat now" appeared on behalf of The National Crime Prevention Council. The ad simultaneously affirmed diversity while positioning Americans as united: all "in the same boat," with hearts "in the same place." But the ad also worked to caution against intolerance. (It was, after all, designed for crime prevention.) In the words of the Ad Council Web site, it "urge[d] Americans that anger should not be directed toward innocent American citizens of different races, cultures, or religions."[6] Interesting here is the echo of a phrasing so often used to describe the victims of 9/11: "innocent Americans." The ad served as a reminder that in the wake of 9/11 intolerance could mirror the terrorism America was committed to fight against. To the conventional phrasing, the PSA added a focus on a unifying citizenship ("innocent American citizens").

A stronger warning was provided by "Racism Can Hide in the Strangest Places. Like Behind Patriotism." Again, a united, patriotic nation was posed, but a dark side of patriotism was made more explicit. In the words of the Ad Council's gloss, "This PSA cautions that during this time of increased patriotism, acts of racism may surface. The ad conveys the message that racism is never acceptable."[7]

**We all came over in different ships,
but we're in the same boat now.**

*Our origins, skin colors or religions may be different,
but our hearts are all in the same place.
Please show tolerance for your fellow Americans.*

Reproduced courtesy of Saatchi & Saatchi,
the National Crime Prevention Council and the Ad Council

**RACISM CAN HIDE IN THE STRANGEST PLACES. LIKE BEHIND PATRIOTISM.**

Reproduced courtesy of the Ad Council

Along with its cautions and exhortations for inclusion, the ad campaign did produce conventionally patriotic ads. An approximation is reproduced opposite, based on the "Pledge of Allegiance" to the U.S. flag. Written in 1892, the pledge is still reportedly recited daily by 60 million American school children,[8] although in 1943 the Supreme Court ruled that the recitation could not be required and the issue continues to be adjudicated.[9]

At the bottom is an image incorporating several of the heraldic elements from the Great Seal of the United States: a bald eagle surmounting a stars-and-stripes shield and grasping a sheaf of arrows in one claw and an olive branch in the other. Beneath that: "September 11, 2001." The intent is unmistakable: "America, one nation, indivisible." But even here, critical readings are possible. The phrase "under God" was added to the pledge late in its history, during the Eisenhower administration and the McCarthy period. Many people continue to feel uncomfortable with it. To quote one patriotic commentator:

Although the flag represents the embodiment of our national conscience and is easily the most recognized symbol of our nation,

I pledge allegiance to the flag

of the United States of America

and to the Republic for which it stands

one nation, under God

# indivisible

with liberty and justice for all.

SEPTEMBER 11, 2001

Reproduced courtesy of Work, Inc. and the Ad Council

one that I proudly support and defend daily as a member of our nation's Armed Forces, I find it curious that a "religious" Pledge of Allegiance to our flag rather than a Pledge of Allegiance to our secular Constitution has become the institutionalized form of patriotism in our country.[10]

Potentially acknowledging discomfort with the pledge, as well as its history, the words *under God* and *flag* are dimmed in comparison to the more secular virtue–*justice*. These complex decisions of how to best unify a diverse nation (of viewers) within secular virtues are best exemplified in one of the council's TV spots.

## I AM AN AMERICAN

Perhaps the most widely circulated ad was the television spot, "I am an American," which seemed to appear almost immediately after 9/11. It was created by staffers of an Austin-based ad agency who'd been in Washington, DC, on September 11. On the long drive home, they hatched the plan for the PSA, which they donated to the Ad Council. The council was able to distribute it to 3,000 media outlets nationwide.[11]

Americans found the PSA very powerful, and beautifully produced. A concise description came from the *Houston Chronicle*:

> The commercial shows people from the melting pot–including a firefighter, children and adults of many ethnicities–facing the camera and saying simply, "I am an American." The screen then flashes the nation's venerable motto, *e pluribus unum*, a Latin phrase that means "out of many, one."[12]

In fact, the ad showed more than 40 individuals–from a nun, to a police officer, to firefighters–with fully diverse skin tones and accents. Some were native speakers of a variety of English dialects, others clearly had first languages other than English. One speaker was in a wheelchair, another used sign language. Speakers stood in urban areas, including New York and San Francisco, as well as in gardens and fields. Each delivery of "I am an American" was a bit different, as the ad captured the variety of individual cadences.

The reaction to the ad was so rich that the Ad Council developed a Web page titled, "What people are saying about 'I am an American'." It is here that we can gain some insight into the varied receptions of this most widely distributed selling of America. We know from media coverage the intent of the ad's makers. It was designed as "a gift to the American people from the advertising industry."[13] Ad agency president, Roy Spence, reported: "We wanted to make sure that when we strike back, we don't strike back at one of our own."[14]

Many of the responses on the "What People are Saying" Web page were laudatory. Here are typical sentiments:

Just thought you'd like to hear about his. I was flying out of Atlanta on Friday, September 28th. Your "I am an American" PSA came on the television monitors as I was passing through a terminal. What followed was something I've never seen in an airport before. I stopped to watch the PSA, and like others was very moved by it. As the PSA played, more and more people stopped to watch. By the time the PSA was over, there were at least 40 people gathered around just the one monitor. With smiles on our faces, we broke up and went about our business. I just want to congratulate you on such a successful campaign and thank you for helping make the day a little bit brighter. (Chris)

Kudos. This ad captures precisely what America should be. I hope it becomes etched in every American's brain. (Robert)

Your "I am an American" television ad stirs the deepest emotions of my American soul. When I see your ad at my age of 40 years it brings tears of sadness and joy to my eyes. Sadness that an unparalleled tragedy had to occur for such an ad to have meaning in our country, but joy in that I think the time may have finally arrived when not just whites and blacks can come together but—all Americans. If I had a million dollars, I'd buy as much ad time as I could for the ad. (Norm)

Thank you for your campaign. The most destructive impact of 9/11 could well be what it turns us into. I believe your campaign will play a part in assuring that we turn into a better nation. Thanks. (Petrops)

Thanks for your ad. Very little air time in the last two weeks has been more valuable. God bless us all. (Franca, Baltimore, MD.)

There is, even in this ad, however, an ambiguity. Does the ad celebrate the achievement of a diverse unity of Americans or is it trying to create this? Put more starkly: Is the ad meant to celebrate or protect nonwhite Americans; does the majority need to be reminded that minorities are members of the community when the wagons are circled? The stated goals of the campaign actually lean toward the latter interpretation—"to assure that we don't strike out at one of our own."

The statements above respond to a rather romanticized viewing. People saw the ad as a reaffirmation of, perhaps a tutorial on, what America could be. But there was a spectrum of responses when viewers rated the ad in its portrayal of diversity. This range of responses indicates that viewers bring with them divergent ingredients from the narrative stew that is public discourse. At the risk of getting carried away with a metaphor: you are what you eat. Many people saw a refreshing range of people on the screen (perhaps because their world is not so diverse?). Within that group, Bob wrote, "It is clear that you intended everyone to be included." Margaret wrote, "the commercial … represents all countries and all types, shapes and colors of faces." Several writers, however, noted limitations on that diversity (perhaps because they are closer to issues of exclusion):

Your PSA is quite powerful and very useful. However, it does not include any Muslim man in Islamic Dress and any Muslim woman in Islamic Dress with the head hijab. Diversification without Muslims is indeed incomplete; Muslims are also American. (Ilyas)

With the recent aftermath of the NY and Washington bombings, male Sikhs in particular and Muslim women have faced the brunt of the backlash. I was hoping that a male Sikh with a turban and beard could be added to this ad. This would speed up the rebuilding process of our great nation and help people understand the differences between various religions and races. (Manny)

I am American and I have been watching your latest campaign on TV with a feeling of admiration, but also a profound feeling of being insulted. You failed to show a single member of the Armed Forces. How utterly thoughtless of you at a time when brave noble brothers and sisters are putting their lives at risk for all of the freedom loving people of this earth. (William)

I love ur ad … it is wonderful … but being an American citizen and wearing a headscarf i don't see myself there pleez have somebody like me too in the ad or if u need assistance i know many people who would be willing to be in it … hope to hear from u sooooon. (Saniya)

These diverse responses confirm that public service announcements, like all texts, are interpreted through a complex interaction of their content and the preexisting perspective of the viewer. Several final responses make this abundantly clear.

I just saw your "I am An American" ad, and while I can appreciate the sentiment, I found it deeply distressing and highly offensive that no European Americans were included in the segment. (Joe)

It is fascinating that fully half the faces (approximately 20) are likely European American. Clearly for viewers who are either unaccustomed to faces of color and/or uncomfortable with these images, it is possible for an equal representation to be completely misperceived. For this viewer, past some threshold, every face became one of color. This is perhaps an extreme example of what is surely universal—seeing ads through the lens of one's particular concerns. One viewer noticed in the ads her "pet peeve":

I really liked your diversity PSA. It addresses a pet peeve of mine. As an Asian American, I find myself constantly correcting my less enlightened Asian friends when they talk about so-and-so's "American" spouse. What do you mean by "American"? Aren't YOU American too? Maybe I can get off the soap box now … thanks. (R. Louie)

The last segments discussed here address assimilation. Randy, of Pennsylvania, wrote of the ads:

They Are The Best!!! Finally, people are standing up and saying that they are Americans, period. Thank you for taking the "hyphen" out of being an American. I never thought it should have been there in the first place. …

It's not the least bit clear that the folks in these ads do not think of themselves as hyphenated Americans, or that they do not take great pride in their ethnic or cultural origins. Nor is it clear that the ad makers intended a message along the lines that to be American, one has to give up hyphenated identities. But for Randy, who was presumably moved by the ad, to assert Americanism is to forego a hyphen.

Earl, from Pennsylvania, saw a distancing from "political correctness" in the ad:

I want to compliment you on your TV ad: "I am an American." After years of insane political correctness it is uplifting to me to see people of different ethnic backgrounds unite as one instead of using hyphens and asking for victim group hand outs. Thankfully, Clinton's "Our strength is our diversity" defiance of common sense did not affect everyone. We do have an American culture, and the nation is strong because the immigrants that came here united in to one people. Your ad reflects my beliefs and I want to thank you for placing it on TV.

Like all viewers, Earl read the ad through the lens of his experience and concerns. While the ad makers might well see "our strength is our diversity" as the perfect gloss for this spot, for Earl the PSA was a corrective to that sentiment. It also appears to Earl to be a denunciation of affirmative action ("victim group hand outs") and an endorsement of assimilation. For other viewers (I daresay most), the ad embraced diversity. Judy wrote from Houston, "Thanks for making Americans aware that 'we' are made up of many nationalities. That's what 'America' is." David, writing from South Carolina, spoke of the "collaboration of our nation's diversity and its unity."

But perhaps the single most important endorsement the Ad Council could have received was Earl's final testimonial, "Your ad reflects my beliefs." In a sense the ad did. It allowed a range of viewers to position themselves as appreciative participants in a racially diverse America. For some viewers that diversity was only visual; they read the ad with an assimilationist tinge. For many others, the ad ratified a society united in its appreciation of diversity. In its ability to allow for both of those readings, "I am an American" became a vehicle for all stripes of patriotism.

David, in Washington, wrote to say that he had responded as "a quiet and grateful patriot." Chris in Canada wrote to say "I haven't seen anything come close, since the tragedy, to expressing so clearly and poignantly what it is we are trying to defend. This ad will cause our enemies consternation." And David, from Pennsylvania, wrote:

> I am a navy veteran of WWII and I still remember the poster with "Loose Lips Sink Ships" on them. I am still impressed with that phrase and happy to learn that you will be adding your know-how to the upcoming struggle. That should help the American people maintain their resolve during the years to come.

While a good deal more complex than "Loose Lips Sink Ships," "I am an American" nonetheless worked the same side of the street: to unite a diverse country in common cause at a time of war. To work "the Arab street" the Bush administration hired an advertising executive to sell the U.S. to the rest of the world. One part of that campaign was the dropping of leaflets over Afghanistan. Examples of that "selling" can be seen on the cover of this book but are beyond its scope.

The Ad Council response to the crisis can be viewed as selling America domestically—selling ideas to it, and selling it to itself. Somewhere along the way, however, America became selling, as Americans were urged to shop their way out of a deepening recession. But the first step was to sell patriotism to a populace that, in recent decades, has not been automatically responsive to such calls.

## PATRIOTISM

In post-9/11 America, "red, white, and blue" was everywhere. Shopping bags and postage stamps boasted flags with the words, "United We Stand"; some bags read "Proud to be American!" Baseball players wore flags on their jersey collars and helmets, "civilians" wore them almost everywhere else. Stores were unable to keep flags in stock;

large magnetic facsimiles were available to place on one's car. Writing in the *Chronicle of Higher Education*, art history professor Karal Ann Marling observed, "The anthem of the hour is Irving Berlin's 'God Bless America'. Taken in conjunction with the news media's images of waving flags, the deity and the Stars and Stripes are merged in an aura of secular religion."[15]

That patriotism was invoked every night on CNN, when Larry King closed his show with a patriotic musical performance. In mid-November, Mary Hampton Callaway (composer of five of Barbra Streisand's songs) sang her newest composition, "I Believe in America." Behind flag-heavy visuals, the last verse extolled the flag, asking Americans to "restore the meaning of the red, white, and blue."

But patriotic campaigns raise concerns. (Chapter 6, "'The New McCarthyism,'" explores the dueling charges of intimidation versus insufficient patriotism that emerged post-9/11.) For a variety of reasons, citizens and organizations began to express their discomfort at the potential legislative correlates of ubiquitous flag waving. In late September the American Civil Liberties Union, together with a broad coalition of more than 150 public policy organizations spanning the political spectrum, issued a ten-point manifesto titled "In Defense of Freedom."[16] It warned of the danger that post-9/11 security measures would compromise fundamental civil liberties.

In "The Greatest Danger Comes from Within," a citizen activist named Jeff Milchen wrote on the Web expressing concerns about government action in times of patriotic fervor. His posting is quoted at some length here, as it echoes frequently expressed concerns raised about a narrowly focused notion of patriotism.[17]

> For me the U.S. flag always stood for freedom above all else. After all, every country on earth has a flag, but none have a Constitution with a Bill of Rights that, despite some failures along the way, has protected the liberty of so many citizens so well, and for so long.
>
> I embraced that symbolism so thoroughly that I founded a non-profit organization with the flag in its logo. ...
>
> My unease made more sense when I recognized that while millions of citizens were waving the Stars and Stripes, our Constitutional

rights were being whittled by Congress' passing legislation that erodes three core protections: freedom of speech, freedom from unreasonable search and seizure, and freedom from deprivation of liberty without due process.

And the flag wavers overwhelmingly were silent.

Milchen expressed concern that "the flag's interpretation had been co-opted to symbolize vengeance or solidarity against an enemy more so than solidarity in defense of freedom." And he warned, "Legislative titles like the 'Patriot Act' (for the [hastily passed law] expanding police … powers) should raise alarm for jingoism." Finally, he observed, "While dangerous laws like the USA Patriot Act already have passed, remember that serious attacks on liberties have occurred in each major war."

A variety of voices continued to echo these alarms. Historian Howard Zinn cautioned that "war is … an opportunity for tighter controls of the country's own population …"[18] Former FBI and CIA director, William Webster, publicly disputed the claim that counter-terrorism operations require expanded surveillance powers.[19] U.S. Representative Bob Barr (R–Georgia) warned that, in passing the USA Patriot Act, Congress had acted in haste,[20] enacting "a massive suspension of civil liberties in a way that has never been done before in our country … likely set[ting] precedents that will come back to haunt us terribly."[21] Others warned against military tribunals.

Thus, a central and persistent issue in the rhetoric of American patriotism returned to the national discourse. What is the proper balance between support for the government in the time of crisis and the preservation of fundamental liberties? Flag waving in the service of a wartime legislative agenda had not gone unnoticed.

But another concern about flag waving was more broadly stated, and linked politics with commerce. Professor Marling observed: "A cynic might be forgiven for thinking that flags are another fashion trend, the latest conspiracy on the part of capitalism to separate honest Americans from their dollars."[22] Flags were the wedge item in the battle for America's pocketbooks. While minority voices worried over civil rights, the majority worried over spending. The battle for the hearts and minds of Americans came to focus on their wallets.

## CONSUMERISM AS PATRIOTISM

The *New York Times* reported that on September 11, 2001, Wal-Mart sold 88,000 American flags, compared with 6,400 on that day a year earlier.[23] But shopping didn't come naturally in the immediate aftermath of the terrorist attacks. "It feels almost disrespectful to come to the store and spend money," a Restoration Hardware shopper was quoted as saying on September 11.[24] This was an attitude that the rhetoric of the Bush administration and retailers would work to overcome.

Americans' reluctance to spend was understandable. The events of September 11 had renewed nonmaterial values. Margaret Carlson wrote in *Time*, "With the collapse of the World Trade Center, the curtain closed on the decade of wretched excess."[25] The contradictions were palpable. On the one hand, Americans were being rhetorically positioned as the heirs of the so-called Greatest Generation. But their task appeared quite different. The *Wall Street Journal* observed, "During World War II, patriotic citizens planted cabbage, collected scrap and lent their money to Uncle Sam. Since the World Trade Center attack, it has been suggested that our patriotic duty now consists of investing in the stock market."[26]

The contradictions emerged again in discussions of war bonds. In late October, the House of Representatives passed a measure to issue savings bonds, as the government had first done to pay for the Civil War. During the Second World War, Americans bought $185 billion in war bonds. The *New York Times* reported that the Treasury Department was "reluctant to support the measure because it fears the bonds will encourage saving and discourage spending." Similarly, "while calling the bill a good patriotic gesture, the Bush administration is not going out of its way to promote the legislation, arguing that in today's economy it is important to encourage consumers to spend."[27]

In a column titled "Patriotic Splurging," Margaret Carlson wrote in *Time*, "The Greatest Generation got to save old tires, dig a Victory Garden and forgo sugar. The Richest Generation is being asked to shop. … The irony of this strange war is that just as we see the limits of what money can buy, buying becomes our patriotic duty."[28]

The car companies launched major media campaigns. In multicultural ads reminiscent of "I am an American," patriotic promotions offered Americans interest-free financing. Americans, so familiar with the phrase "Let's Roll"—the final words of Flight 93 hero Todd Beamer—would see

Saturn ads telling them to "visit your Saturn retailer and 'Keep America Rolling'." To buy a Chevy was to "Keep America Rolling Forward." Ford was more explicit in linking its TV ads to the events of 9/11:

In an instant everything can change. Yet everywhere you look the spirit of America is alive. That spirit makes us what we are today and what we will be tomorrow. We at Ford want to celebrate that spirit with the Ford Drives America Program, to help America move forward with interest-free financing on all new Fords.

Ford was "help[ing] America" to "move forward" (to heal). Ford would help Americans do their patriotic duty. Patriotism had become consumerism.

By Christmas, people began returning to the stores. "I am a patriot, not a debtor," Jeff Rundles wrote in *Colorado Business*. "Not exactly a firefighter or anything, but a hero of sorts. An American patriot. I went out this Christmas and spent like there was no tomorrow so that I might be responsible for the recession ending earlier than predicted, or the Taliban being defeated, or something else really important to the country."[29] But Rundles didn't consume without regret: "A little voice inside me still keeps repeating that it is better to give than to receive, volunteerism is better than consumerism, and we need more compassion, not more greed."

The Ad Council's campaign had begun with the premise that Americans needed each other. The calendar year ended with another kind of campaign, one designed to once again persuade Americans that they needed things.

## NOTES

1  Ad Council of America, "Message From the President of the Ad Council of America," www.adcouncil.org/crisis/index.htm.
2  Claire Cozens, "American Ad Body in Call to Arms," *Guardian Unlimited*, October 2, 2001.
3  Greg Hassell, "Altruistic Ads Try to Unite Americans," *Houston Chronicle*, September 25, 2001.
4  Ad Council.
5  Ibid.
6  Available www.adcouncil.org/crisis/print.htm.

7   Ibid.
8   Ken Lynn, "The Origin ad Meaning of the Pledge of Allegiance." Available www.ffrf.org/fttoday/may99/lynn.html.
9   See, for example, www.aclu-wa.org/issues/students/PledgeLetter.html.
10  Lynn.
11  Hassell.
12  Ibid.
13  Ibid.
14  Ibid.
15  Karal Ann Marling, "Stars and Stripes, American Chamleon," *The Chronicle of Higher Education/The Chronicle Review*, October 26, 2001.
16  "In Defense of Freedom." Available www.indefenseoffreedom.org.
17  Jeff Milchen, "The Greatest Danger Comes from Within," *Common Dreams Newscenter: Breaking News & Views for the Progressive Community*, November 17, 2001. Available www.commondreams.org/views01/1117-05.htm.
18  Howard Zinn, "Born Yesterday," *Tikkun*, May/June 2002, p. 32.
19  Robert D. Romero, "ACLU Insists on Need to be Safe and Free"(ACLU Press Release), ACLU Freedom Network. Available www.aclu.org/news/2002/n020602b.html.
20  Joe Geshwiler, "Panel Faults Restrictions Imposed Since September 11," *Atlanta Journal-Constitution*, April 4, 2002.
21  Nat Hentoff, "Getting Back Our Rights," *Village Voice*, December 7, 2001.
22  Marling.
23  Blaine Harden and Leslie Kaufman, "Mood of Sellers and Buyers, as Well as Purchases, Reflect the Devastating Events," *New York Times*, September 13, 2001.
24  Ibid.
25  Margaret Carlson, "Patriotic Splurging," *Time*, October 15, 2001.
26  Roger Lowenstein, "Don't Let Patriotism Dull the Market's Edge," *Wall Street Journal*, September 19, 2001.
27  Information on war bonds comes from Lizette Alvarez, "House passes a War-Bond Bill, but Bush is Not Enthusiastic," *New York Times*, October 26, 2001.
28  Carlson.
29  Jeff Rundles, "Paying for Patriotism," *Colorado Business*, January 2002.

# 6

# "The New McCarthyism"

Along with increased patriotism, post-9/11 saw attacks on those who questioned U.S. policy. A provoking volley was fired by the conservative American Council of Trustees and Alumni (ACTA). Founded in 1995 by Lynne Cheney, wife of the Vice President, ACTA functions as a watchdog group to monitor and influence higher education. In November, ACTA published a report listing more than 100 examples of what it claimed was a "blame America first" attitude on America's campuses. "We were struck by the moral cleavage that exists between the intellectual elites and mainstream America" the group's vice president, Anne Neal, is quoted as saying.[1] While ACTA tarred campuses as a "weak link," some on campus moved toward different analogies. Psychology Professor David Barash transformed the ACTA acronym to signify the "Arbitrary Committee for the Talibanization of America, or Academe."[2] This chapter follows the ACTA campaign and reactions to it.

## NAMING

Probably the most troubling aspect of the ACTA report was its naming of names. This proved too reminiscent of the right's blacklisting legacy under Joe McCarthy, and many were quick to make the connection. One e-list discussed the report under the heading "Lynne Cheney's Got Her Little List."[3] A more trenchant commentary by anthropologist David Price appeared in *Counterpunch*, under the title, "Academia Under Attack: Sketches for a New Blacklist." It began, "My office is cluttered with over 20,000 pages of FBI files chronicling the damage inflicted on academic freedom in America by McCarthyism. These hundreds of different files tell divergent stories with various twists and turns and morals, but most of them are bound together by a simple feature: the names of these individuals whose lives were invaded and altered appeared somewhere. ..." The outcry against ACTA's "blacklist" proved sufficiently great that within days its Web site had removed names, producing (in the whimsical description of one critic) "an anonymous graylist."[4] (The original report, however, is archived in several locations on the Internet.)

For linguists, the concept of the *performative* is operative here. Some utterances bring things into being simply through their performance. A commonplace example occurs through uttering the phrase "I now pronounce you husband and wife." Through the performance of that language, the legal status of individuals is changed. During the McCarthy period in the United States, lists acted as a kind of performative. Listing performed a system of guilt by association; to be named was to be "blacklisted."

## THE LIST

ACTA's list is presented as an appendix to its report, *Defending Civilization*. The offending quotes (generally one to two sentences in length) were taken from published reports of college teach-ins and rallies as well as from Internet sites. Two entries were later omitted, one made by a conservative faculty member who felt that he'd been "hit by friendly fire" and who declared, "no one should have a license to hunt unpatriotic speech."[5] Many of the citations are noteworthy for their innocuousness. Former Deputy Secretary of State Strobe Talbot (now Director of Yale's Center for the Study of Globalization) is fingered for "It is from the desperate, angry and bereaved that these suicide pilots came." Jesse Jackson was quoted in a speech at Harvard, "[We should] build bridges and relationships, not simply bombs and walls." A Stanford professor made the list with "If Osama Bin Laden is confirmed to be behind the attacks, the United States should bring him before an international tribunal on charges of crimes against humanity."

Some citations made easy targets, none more so than a statement by historian Richard Berthold, more typically a critic of the left. He immediately apologized for saying, "Anyone who can blow up the Pentagon gets my vote," indicating that it was a "stupid, pathetic attempt at a joke."[6] Most entries, however, were considerably less incendiary. Grouping statements within a few categories will give us some sense of what constitutes being a "weak link" in ACTA-speak. In the discussion below, citations from the *Defending Civilization* appendix are cited with their position on its numbered list. Except in identified excerpts, all ellipses and editing appear as in the ACTA report. By way of context, three-quarters of the quotes occurred before the beginning of U.S. air strikes on Afghanistan, almost all before it was clear that the initial assaults would be carefully targeted. At that historical moment, ACTA framed peaceniks as blameworthy, as indicated in the following entries:

26. "[B]reak the cycle of violence."

27. "We have to learn to use courage for peace instead of war."

30. "What do we want? Peace! When do we want it? Now!" [Harvard rally chant]

112. "Stop the violence, stop the hate."

89. "War created people like Osama bin Laden, and more war will create more people like him."

In terms of sheer number of citations, a particularly robust category comprised statements that called for analysis and education (particularly from a historical perspective), or strategic thinking:

38. ... "In this time of crisis, we have an unusual opportunity to see past stereotypes, identify and diminish our own prejudices, and experience a complex world through the sensitivities of others. ..." (excerpt)

49. "[I]gnorance breeds hate."

63. "[We] need to hear more than one perspective on how we can make the world a safer place. We need to understand the reasons behind the terrifying hatred directed against the United States and find ways to act that will not foment more hatred for generations to come."

64. "[D]emocracies, because they have a sense of self-pride and moral consciousness, can often act without restraint and be destructive of

the values they are trying to promote. The thinking is to find the perpetrators and engage in a military response and feel that that solves something. But there needs to be an understanding of why this kind of suicidal violence could be undertaken against our country."

77. "We need to think about what could have produced the frustrations that caused these crimes. To have that kind of hatred is a phenomenon we will have to try to understand."

78. "The question we should explore is not who we should bomb or where we should bomb, but why we were targeted. When we have the answer to why, then we will have the ability to prevent terrorist attacks tomorrow."

105. "Contingent Predictions: ... Bombing the presumed originator(s) of Tuesday's attacks and forcing other countries to choose sides will therefore aggravate the very conditions American leaders will declare they are preventing. ... If so, democracy (defined as relatively broad and equal citizenship, binding consultation of citizens, and protection from arbitrary actions by governmental agents) will decline across the world."

Another category of dangerous speech criticized the escalating rhetoric of the day.

32. "[I deplore those] who are deploying rhetoric and deploying troops without thinking before they speak."

37. "... The responsible thing for the President and Congress to do would be to lower the rhetorical temperature in Washington and halt the contest to sound more bellicose and patriotic than the last politician or official ..." (excerpt)

74. "To declare war, in this case, is a dangerous use of metaphoric language: it dignifies terrorist acts and implies a war with terrorists could end with a peace treaty. We must resist calls for revenge or retaliation."

91. "The media has stirred the country into a froth of hatred and revenge. ..." (excerpt)

Coming so soon after the September 11 attacks, some speakers cautioned against vengeance:

> 33/52. "An eye for an eye makes the world blind." (This adaptation from Gandhi is cited on placards at both Harvard and the University of North Carolina.)
>
> 65. "Our grief is not a cry for war."
>
> 74. "… We must resist calls for revenge or retaliation." (excerpt)

And, of course, all statements were taken out of context. According to the *New York Times*,[7] Todd Gitlin made the list by responding to a journalist's query concerning the mood at New York University. ACTA entry no. 68 (September 21, 2001) has Gitlin replying, "There is a lot of skepticism about the administration's policy of going to war." In some profound irony, Gitlin—a sixties protester—makes ACTA's "short on patriotism" list at a moment when he has draped an American flag across his Manhattan balcony.[8]

In hindsight, one realizes that many of these comments made in the searching moments after September 11 were prescient. At Pomona College, a "faculty panel discussing U.S. obligations in the Mideast" was cited for advocating that we "break the cycle of violence"—a position the Bush administration later embraced. Calls to understand the making of the terrorists were answered by a PBS Frontline documentary, "Inside the Terror Network." And a student comment, "Poverty breeds resentment and resentment breeds anger" was echoed by President Bush in his March 22, 2002, remarks at the United Nation's Financing for Development Conference in Monterrey, Mexico: "We fight against poverty because hope is an answer to terror." But what was most apparent at the time was the potentially chilling effect of the report. It was not the citations alone that made the report dangerous. It was the document that accompanied them.

## THE REPORT

The argument structure of the report goes something like the following. In the wake of September 11, popular polls and statements by politicians (termed "leaders") have unequivocally supported the President and the policy of military action in Afghanistan. In contrast, university faculty are said to have equivocated, thus "proving a shocking divide between academe and the public at large." Public statements from professors are critiqued for being insufficiently patriotic, rendering faculty "the weak link" in America's response to terror. Their "self-flagellation" sends the message, "blame America first." The faculty's "moral relativism" creates an attack on Western civilization and an atmosphere "increasingly unfriendly to the free exchange of ideas." Evidence of this attack is seen in the addition of courses on Islamic and Asian cultures. For the West to survive, colleges and universities must adopt a core curriculum including Western civilization and American history (a call that characterizes ACTA's ongoing agenda).

We'll begin by looking closely at the ACTA report, *Defending Civilization: How our Universities are Failing America*. Throughout the report, its defense of American civilization is linked directly to the ongoing war effort. Arguably, conflating war with a defense of civilization also links the report to the Bush administration's analysis of the terrorist attacks. By this construal, the attacks did not target government policy, but rather American civilization and its very way of life. Many responses found the report "chilling." If the military defends American civilization against outside forces, by analogy is the report defending against threats from the inside? "Boring from within," of course, was the charge of the McCarthy period—the concept that leftists had infiltrated America's institutions. "Policing the Academy" was how one headline characterized the report.[9] "Academia Under Attack" read another.[10] Was the War on Terrorism to be accompanied by a war on academia? The report was certainly experienced that way. Note the military metaphors in this report from the *San Jose Mercury News*: "An aggressive attack on freedom has been launched upon America's college campuses. Its perpetrators seek the elimination of ideas and activities that place Sept. 11 in historical context, or critique the so-called war on terrorism."[11]

A closer look at the report itself will explain these alarms. As usual, I will be particularly interested in the way the language of the report creates a post-9/11 world. Written under the names of the organization's President and Vice President (Jerry L. Martin and Anne D. Neal, respectively) it begins with an October quote from "founder and chairman emeritus" United States Second Lady Lynne V. Cheney:

At a time of national crisis, I think it is particularly apparent that we need to encourage the study of our past. Our children and grandchildren—indeed all of us—need to know the idea and ideals on which our nation has been built. We need to understand how fortunate we are to live in freedom. We need to understand that living in liberty is such a precious thing that generations of men and women have been willing to sacrifice everything for it. We need to know, in a war, exactly what is at stake.

Notwithstanding the early successes of the War on Terrorism, the report announces a nation in "crisis," apparently because of some form of amnesia. The problem seems to lie in educational institutions. As we have seen in previous chapters, a powerful ability of language is to signal which information is "given," that is, old information, and to mark that which is "new." The repeated litany here indicating "*the need* to understand" suggests that this is new information: the collective readership somehow does not understand how fortunate it is to live in freedom, that freedom is hard-won, and why exactly they are at war. The solution to this pressing need, we'll discover later, comes in the form of ACTA's mandate to study history and "core curricula."

Another role of language is the creation of identity. Prominent in the epigram is an "us" that implies a "them," a division that would play out dramatically in subsequent pages.

An interesting aspect of the report's subtitle is the notion of academic "grading," that universities have "failed" America. The document itself, however, reads like a failed exercise in basic logic. Throughout this discussion, I'll be indexing the locations of common logical fallacies.[12]

The first occurs in Cheney's opening sentence: "At a time of national crisis, I think it is particularly apparent that we need to encourage the study of our past." *Circulus in probando* occurs when one assumes as a premise the conclusion that one wishes to reach. The need to study the past, in this framing, becomes both premise and conclusion. And not only are premise and conclusion conflated in this sentence; ironically, this fallacy structures the report as a whole as it both begins (with premise) and ends (concludes) with this same quotation.

After the epigram, we move into the report proper:

In the wake of the September 11 terrorist attacks, Americans across the country responded with anger, patriotism, and support of military intervention. The polls have been nearly unanimous—92% in favor of military force even if casualties occur—and citizens have rallied behind the President wholeheartedly.

*Argumentum ad numerum,* our second logical fallacy, occurs when arguments are made on the basis of numbers, on the assumption that the more people support something the more likely it is to be correct. With 92% supporting military force, it must be right. (It is probably worth noting here that a Gallup Poll released on September 21 indicated that only 54% of Americans supported launching an attack when that option was placed against "extraditing the terrorists to stand trial."[13]) *Argumentum ad veracundium* is our next lapse: the appeal to authority. "Rallying behind the President" is a call for tactical unity masquerading as correctness of analysis: If the President supports it, it must certainly be right.

In contrast to "Americans across the country" is the academy:

> Not so academe. Even as many institutions enhanced security and many students exhibited American flags, college and university faculty have been the weak link in America's response to the attack. Proving a shocking divide between academe and the public at large, professors across the country sponsored teach-ins that typically ranged from moral equivocation to explicit condemnations of America.

Continuing the bifurcation of *us* and *them,* "academe"—positioned previously against "Americans"—is now contrasted to "the public." And, in a deployment of incendiary language, academics are characterized as a "weak link," a phrase used by McCarthyism's House Un-American Activities Committee to describe a scientist it had targeted.[14] It is from this use of language (along with the naming) that many of the accusations of McCarthyism arise. The incendiary language (sometimes discussed under "vice and virtue words" in beginning logic discussions[15] continues with a *shocking* divide between faculty and others, a divide that is characterized by "*moral equivocation*" or "*condemnations* of America" (italics added). This is a complicated claim to disentangle logically. On the one hand is the implication that moral lapses and condemnations characterize the statements we have before us. As we've seen above, one person's moral lapse is another's call for sanity. On the other hand is the suggestion that these statements are "typical" of observations made at forums across the nation. The logical fallacy here is one of *hasty generalizations*: a general rule is derived from specific cases that aren't necessarily representative. Note that fewer than half of the statements are attributed to faculty at all; many are attributed to signs, slogans, and guest speakers; and 25 come from the same two institutions, many from the same events. The *New York Times* quoted an MIT faculty member reporting that "'Three of the four quotes they used come from a peace rally on campus. ... But there were at least six other panels, and a majority of people who spoke at those panels didn't criticize American foreign policy.' He added, 'One of my colleagues has called for a resumption of government-sponsored assassination'."[16]

A similar logical structure appears in the next paragraph, but with an additional twist.

> While America's elected officials from both parties and media commentators from across the spectrum condemned the attacks and followed the President in calling evil by its rightful name, many faculty demurred. Some refused to make judgments. Many invoked tolerance and diversity as antidotes to evil. Some even pointed accusatory fingers, not at that the terrorists, but at America itself.

Again, we have faculty positioned against authorities, in this case "elected officials," "media commentators," and "the President." Here, it is the grammar of the paragraph that positions the faculty. While authorities did X, many faculty did *not-X*. Some did *not-X_1*. Many did *not-X_2*. Some even did *not-X_3*. Clearly, if what the authorities did is good, what "some/ many" faculty did was bad. Some "even" did something really bad. In a sense, what the faculty are accused of doing is being faculty members. They withheld judgment, the hallmark of good research, and invoked tolerance and diversity. They didn't say the obvious (killing innocent people is evil), because their task is to go beyond the obvious.[17] Since they weren't operating within an "evil" framework, it's hard to know how they could possibly have done what they are excoriated for doing: to invoke tolerance and diversity as antidotes to evil. We will return to "the accusatory finger" later.

What follows next are three quotes under the heading "Leaders from Both Parties":

President George W. Bush: "In this conflict, there is no neutral ground. If any government sponsors the outlaws and killers of innocents, they have become outlaws and murderers, themselves. And they will take that lonely path at their own peril."

Joint Statement by Senate Majority Leader Tom Daschle and Minority Leader Trent Lott: "What happened on Tuesday, September 11th, was not simply an attack against America. It was a crime against democracy, and decency. It was a crime against humanity."

New York City Mayor Rudolph Giuliani: "This was not just an attack on the City of New York or on the United States of America. It was an attack on the very idea of a free, inclusive, and civil society. ... On one side is democracy, the rule of law, and respect for human life; on the other is tyranny, arbitrary executions, and mass murder. We're right and they're wrong. It's a simple as that."

Recall the claim on the table that colleges and universities are characterized by equivocation. In contrast, in these quotes "there is no neutral ground." There is "respect for human life" and there are "crimes against humanity." A quite terrible analogy is at least suggested between rogue states that support terrorists and rogue academics who equivocate. And in both cases the logical fallacy is one of *bifurcation*, that within a complex situation there exist only two options.

As a side bar beneath the quotes is ACTA's characterization of campus comments:

Many invoked tolerance and diversity as antidotes to evil. Some even pointed accusatory fingers, not at the terrorists, but at America itself.

A slippery slope is thus implied between tolerance of other perspectives and accusations toward America. It is the accusations that presumably appear under the next heading, "Voices on Campus." Having already noted the logical flaw in basing claims on unrepresentative quotations taken out of context, I'll quote just one.

> Hugh Gusterson, professor of anthropology and science and technology studies, Massachusetts Institute of Technology: "[I]magine the real suffering and grief of people in other countries. The best way to begin a war on terrorism might be to look in the mirror."

It's easy to see why ACTA chose to highlight this quotation; it does after all suggest that policy makers "look in the mirror." Gusterson was later interviewed by Sharon Basco on the Web site *TomPaine.com*. I'll quote Gusterson at length, since it can be quite helpful in analyzing language use to hear from the speaker. He begins by discussing what it means to take language out of context.

> One interesting thing I want to observe about that quote is where they chose to begin it. It's a quote from a speech I made at a peace rally at MIT, shortly after September 11th. And I took as my theme the difficulty of imagining the real suffering of other people. And just before that quote they select, I talked about how difficult it is for us to imagine the suffering of the people at the World Trade Center as they were dying. And then I went on from there to invite the audience to try and imagine the suffering of people in Afghanistan if we are to go and declare war on the people of Afghanistan. Of course, the quote is carefully cut so it seems that I only care about the suffering of people in other countries and not about the suffering of Americans as well. …

After noting what we might call this *fallacy of exclusion* (leaving out evidence that might change the outcome), Gusterson speaks to the issue of campus discourses—the nature of the conversation in which one takes a turn in campus forums.

> I'd like to make a point that universities are not adjuncts of the American government. The role and the purpose of the university in America is not to cheer-lead for whatever the chosen policy of the American government is. The role and purpose of the university is to pursue knowledge and to encourage people to think critically.

Even with these clarifications, we have insufficient context to interpret the phrase "to look in the mirror." We still have neither a clear sense of Gusterson's intent, nor how the comment was likely to be heard in the context of his full remarks and the remarks of others that day. Gusterson might mean that to understand suffering we have to imagine our own. Or he might mean that of all the actions we will need to take to combat the evil of terrorism, one will be to consider U.S. government actions that are experienced in other nations as creating terror. Or the phrase could have a myriad of other meanings. One may not like the critical stance suggested by this fragment, but the phrase does not "blame America," which is the next charge leveled.

Following the "Voices" quotes is one of the most oft-cited segments of the report:

> Rarely did professors publicly mention heroism, rarely did they discuss the difference between good and evil, the nature of Western political order or the virtue of a free society. Their public messages were short on patriotism and long on self-flagellation. Indeed, the message of much of academe was clear: BLAME AMERICA FIRST.

The term *rarely* generates yet another *hasty generalization*, that is, a quantitative generalization that would be impossible to make based on these 117 single utterances made by fewer than 60 faculty members. How can we know what each of several hundred thousand faculty members at institutions of higher education might have said with respect to the events of September 11?

The first sentence is of such disputable relevance in the context of forums on international policy that it may fairly be considered a *red herring*. Is one indictable for not discussing the ACTA agenda in discussions of international events? Why would one discuss heroism in a public forum on an arguably unrelated topic? The answer seems to come in the next sentence: "Their public messages were short on patriotism and long on self-flagellation."

In English we assume that two sentences that appear together will share a logical relationship if at all possible. This is described as "contiguity implies causation." So for example, if we see the sentence *It was cold in the room* followed by *Jane closed the window*, we will assume that Jane closed the window because it was cold. In some languages, this relationship must be marked, for example, **Because** *it was cold, Jane closed the window*. In English this marking is optional; we assume a relationship unless proved otherwise. Thus, the reader is led to assume that there is a relationship between being "short on patriotism" and rarely mentioning, heroism, good/evil, the Western political order, and the virtue of a free society. *Patriotism*, through its placement, is indexed by discussion of heroism, evil, Western civilization and a free society. Patriotism, in short, is ACTA. In contrast is "self-flagellation," which "indeed" is glossed as blaming America first.

Space does not allow the careful reading of each of the succeeding paragraphs, so we will move quickly through the remainder of the document. A sidebar announces the major argument in the next paragraph:

> And while professors should be passionately defended in their right to academic freedom, that does not exempt them from criticism. The fact remains that academe is the only sector of American society that is distinctly divided in its response.

The allusion to academic freedom will become important in the response to the document, which will be discussed below. What is interesting here is "the fact remains"—a phrase that introduces an undeniable indictment. And the crime? Academe is divided. Rather than celebrate the diversity of opinion, the document problematizes "division" itself. Division within the academy serves to divide the academy from the American "us." Higher education, thus, becomes a weak link by virtue of its free exchange of ideas.

But the document is more complex and, at this stage, filled with contradictions that we won't have time to visit in detail. Two perplexing contradictions are worthy of note as they characterize the intellectual climate on campus. First, the academy is simultaneously criticized for being "divided in its response," while at the same time claimed to have "an atmosphere increasingly unfriendly to the free exchange of ideas." It is, of course, hard to see how public divisions (claimed to be more pervasive than in any other sector of society) can exist outside an exchange of ideas. A second contradiction comes with respect to ideology. On the one hand the document acknowledges that "*most* faculty presumably shared America's horror and condemnation of the terrorist attacks"; at the same time, the document claims that there is a "*dominant* campus ideology" to the contrary (italics added). This ideology, the reader has already been told, is "short on patriotism."

The document goes on to link the lack of patriotism on campuses to a lack of instruction in Western civilization ("the civilization under attack") and American history. It quotes Lynne Cheney in critiquing the study of non-Western texts, "'To say that it is more important now [to study Islam] implies that the events of Sept. 11 were our fault, that it was our failure … that led to so many deaths and so much destruction'." But the basis of this implication is never made clear: What is it that implies that the study of Islam renders September 11 "our fault"? By this logic (and the linkage of fault to blame to patriotism), has the study of Islam become unpatriotic?

The establishment of a core curriculum and the study of American history were central tenets of ACTA's mission well before September 11. In the report, these have been offered as antidotes to what are termed "*trendy* classes and *incoherent* requirements that do not convey the *great* heritage of human civilization" (italics of vice and virtue words added). Ironically, references to history abound on the ACTA list. What is apparently absent from the ACTA perspective, however, is a particular view of history—one could argue that the statements fail to ratify a single, received view of the past.

Towards the end of the report, the invocation of history becomes chilling: Our close reading will end with the penultimate paragraph:

We learn from history that when a nation's intellectuals are unwilling to defend its civilization, they give aid and comfort to its adversaries. In 1933, the Oxford Student Union held a famous debate over whether it was moral for Britons to fight for king and country. After a wide-ranging discussion in which the leading intellectuals could find no distinction between British colonialism and world fascism, the Union resolved that England would "in no circumstances fight for king and country." As the *Wall Street Journal* reported: "Von Ribbentrop sent back the good news to Germany's new chancellor, Hitler: The West will not fight for its own survival."

We believe that the West will fight for its own survival. But only if we know what we are fighting for.

"We learn from history that when a nation's intellectuals are unwilling to defend its civilization, they give aid and comfort to its adversaries." At this stage our nation's intellectuals are a single word short of the U.S. Constitution's definition of treason: "to give aid and comfort to the enemy." And through *false analogy*, today's intellectuals are likened to the British fascists of 1933. Without the ACTA academic agenda, that is, unless we know what we're fighting for, today's faculty are in danger of sending the same message that was sent to "'Hitler: The West will not fight for its own survival'."

The conflation of dissent with lack of patriotism and treason caused a firestorm of response.

## THE RESPONSE

Some of the responses were mocking. Lani Silver wrote in the *San Francisco Examiner*:

Dear Mrs. Cheney:
I write in hopes that you and the organization you co-founded, the American Council of Trustees and Alumni, will add me to your list of 117 liberal academics who have offended you with their so-called anti-American comments.

If you'd add my name to your list, I'd be able to stand alongside some of the people I most respect—people like sociologist Todd Gitlin of NYU. Gitlin made the list when a reporter asked him to describe the mood on his campus and he replied, "There is a lot of skepticism about the administration's policy of going to war."

Off with his head!

Professor Joel Belnin of Stanford made the list for saying: "If Osama bin Laden is confirmed to be behind the attacks, the U.S. should bring him before an international tribunal on charges of crimes against humanity."

Seditious bastard ...[18]

Quoted in the *Boulder Weekly*, Professor Erin Carlston from the University of North Carolina at Chapel Hill writes "I can fervently affirm that I am every bit as treasonous as (my colleagues on the list)." Carlson ends by affirming her dedication to reasoned debate and independent thinking, and asks, "please include me on any future blacklists you choose to publish."[19]

*The Nation* published a compendium of statements by Americans asking to be on the list, entitled "Tattletales for an Open Society."[20]

Perhaps partially in response to ACTA's caricaturing of campus discussion, in February, a group of "prominent American scholars" released a subtly argued 16-page statement in support of military action based on the principles of a "just war."[21]

Some of the responses to the report came in the form of corrections. Additional professors and administrators came forward to protest the snippits of their speech that appeared on the ACTA list. Some of these were staunch supporters of military action in Afghanistan and resented the misrepresentation. Critics noted that the ACTA analysis did not account for the conservative nature of university students: "Recent polls of college kids demonstrate that they are pretty conservative and supportive of the war. So if their teachers are engaged in a covert plot to indoctrinate them into a dangerous Leftist cult, it ain't working."[22]

Other corrections came with respect to misrepresentations of events portrayed on the ACTA list. And in contrast to ACTA's suggestion that liberalism is protected speech on campus, the press began to report sanctions on dissident voices. Thousands of professors signed email statements in support of academic freedom. And, in perhaps the most impressive stand for free speech, a group of faculty members from Florida universities wrote in support of a colleague who had been fired by the (largely Jeb Bush-appointed) board of trustees because of the "disruption" his remarks had caused his university. They wrote:

> By the principles upon which this Nation was founded, each person has the right to speak—indeed is encouraged to speak—as an individual. And a scholar has a greater obligation to be honest than to be agreeable. Therefore, while we have varied opinions on what Professor Al-Arian says, we defend his right to speak. We believe that only out of a debate that includes all voices will the truth come forth.[23]

Indeed, the most robust debate came within the contested terrain of "free speech."

## DUELING HEADLINES/DUELING TEXTS

"Lynne Cheney-Joe Lieberman Group Puts Out a Blacklist" warned the *San Jose Mercury News.*"[24] "Is it 'Blacklisting' or Mere Criticism?" the conservative *National Journal* seemed to reply.[25] The Ayn Rand Institute's "America's Intellectuals: Our most Dangerous Enemy"[26] was met with L.A. Independent Media Collective's description, "Attacking the Academy in the Name of Saving It."[27]

Just as campuses braced to defend their right to dissent, the conservative press accused them of endangering free speech. "The pot calling the kettle black,"[28] was one dissenter's description. And Web sites called attention to this typical use of propaganda: to accuse one's enemies of one's own acts. But the waters had been muddied. Note the similarities between the following two texts. The first is a defense of the academy against "rightwing pundits"; the second, a defense of conservatives.

> Everyone professes to love free speech—the president of the University of Texas calls it the "bedrock of American liberty." The American council for Trustees and Alumni supports it. The mayor of Modesto defends it. The president of the University of Florida applauds it. All are committed to free speech. Just not on their dime, not on their campus, not in their backyard. Not when it disrupts or upsets.[29]

As professors from across the country have spoken out on the events of September 11, the issue of academic freedom has become the focus of intense public debate. Several higher education associations and media editorialists have come forth in support of freedom of speech on campus. We welcome their support for a position we have long maintained. We deplore, however, their silence or complicity over many years as intolerance of dissenting views on our campuses became the norm. Speech and harassment codes, intimidation of speakers, theft of campus newspapers, and other coercive mechanisms have artificially created bland and predictable public orthodoxies where intellectual debate and diversity once existed.[30]

Even the poet Auden is pressed into service for contrasting perspectives. Conservative Norman Podhoretz accepts the premise that America's institutions and way of life have been under attack from within. He traces the responses to September 11 to the activism of the 1960s, analogizing contemporary and sixties activists to those who defended fascism in the 1930s. Here is his quote from Auden's "September 1, 1939."

> I sit on one of the dives
> On Fifty-second Street
> Uncertain and afraid
> As the clever hopes expire
> Of a low dishonest decade

Paul Rosenberg cites a different verse of the same poem, hypothesizing that were Auden alive today the following lines would have made the ACTA list for blaming America first:

> I and the public know
> What all schoolchildren learn:
> Those to whom evil is done
> Do evil in return

The ACTA document manufactures an attack on civilization that parallels the terrorist attack on America. Its defense is the ACTA agenda—restricted ("core") curricula and the study of a received version of history—along with an attack on unpatriotic speech. It has likely been a positive result that targets of the ACTA attacks as well as ACTA's defenders both rely on a discourse of academic freedom. But we are a long way from seeing engaged debate.

As the New Year approached, ACTA's star was no longer in ascendance. Two factors explain its declining fortunes. The first is that the routing of the Taliban in Afghanistan went a great deal more swiftly than many civilians would have predicted, and the reported civilian casualties seemed low. Campuses were a great deal less active. A second phenomenon may be characteristic of "witch hunts." As had been the case in Salem, Massachusetts, 300 years before, ACTA had simply gone too far in its naming of (distinguished) names and its implied attack on free speech. Gone were the heady days of the 2000 presidential campaign when the *New York Times* had reported ACTA's heyday: "No matter which party wins, so does the council ... Both Mrs. Cheney and Mr. Lieberman were among its founders five years ago. 'These are not just two members of our council, but our two most active members ...'" Notwithstanding the use of Lynne Cheney's writing to frame the document, and her status as founder and "Chairman Emeritus," it became widely reported that she had distanced herself from the report, claiming she had not been involved in its development. Democrat Joe Lieberman went further. On December 18, 2001, he released a letter written to ACTA Chair Jerry Martin:

In the past, the Council has often sent me advanced copies of its publications before they have been released and asked for my support. In this case, though, I was never given the opportunity to review the Defending Civilization report before it was made public. I first learned of it through a call to my office from a reporter in Connecticut about a controversy the report had stirred at Wesleyan University.

If I had been given an advanced copy, I would have objected to its content and methodology and asked you either to revise it or make clear that I had no involvement with it. But because that did not happen, and because I have been incorrectly listed on your website as a co-founder of the Council, a number of news accounts and commentaries have associated me with the report and incorrectly asserted or implied that I endorse it.

This letter is meant to set the record straight about my disapproval of this report, which I consider unfair and inconsistent for an organization devoted to promoting academic freedom. To avoid any future confusion, I would ask you to remove any reference to me as a "co-founder" of ACTA from your website or other Council documents. And I would ask that you note in any future public statements that I do not support this specific report. Thank you."

The ACTA report had taken the "culture wars" to a new level. What had been a "War of Words" became a "War on Words." But, lest we assume ACTA had been bested, it's worth considering that it had gained a degree of media exposure well beyond the reach of most watchdog groups.

## NOTES

1 Stuart Eskenazi, "Academic Freedom is Under Attack Since Sept. 11, Some Professors Say," *The Seattle Times*, December 17, 2001.
2 Ibid.
3 http://lists.elistx.com/archives/interesting-people/200112/msg0315.html
4 Eric Scigliano, "Naming—and Un-Naming—Names," *The Nation*, December 31, 2001.
5 Eskenazi.
6 Gia Fenoglia, "Is it 'Blacklisting' or Mere Criticism?" *National Journal*, January 19, 2002.
7 Emily Eakin, "An Organization on the Lookout for Patriotic Incorrectness," *New York Times*, November 24, 2001.
8 Ibid.
9 Eric Alterman, "Policing the Academy," *MSNBC*, November 29, 2001. Available http://lists.village.virginia.edu/lists_archive/sixties-1/3848.html.
10 David Price, "Academia Under Attack: Sketches for a New Blacklist," *Counterpunch*, November 21, 2001.
11 Roberto J. Gonzales, "Lynne Cheney-Joe Lieberman Groups Puts Out a Blacklist," *San Jose Mercury News*, December 13, 2001.
12 Definitions of logical fallacies listed in this chapter are taken from Madsen Pirie, *The Book of the Fallacy*, Routledge, 1985, and W. Ward Fearnside & William B. Holther, *Fallacy: The Counterfeit of Argument*, Prentice-Hall, 1959.
13 Gallup International, "Gallup International Poll on Terrorism in the US (figures)." Available www.gallup-international.com/terrorismpoll_figures.htm, September 21, 2001.
14 Michelle Chihara, "The Silencing of Dissent: Free Speech is too Expensive for Some," *The Boulder News*, January 3, 2002.

15  Michelle Chihara, "The Silencing of Dissent: Free Speech is too Expensive for Some," *The Boulder News,* January 3, 2002.

16  Joy M. Reid, *The Process of Composition,* Prentice-Hall, 1982. p. 104.

17  Eakin.

18  This observation is also made by Paul H. Rosenberg in "Picking Apart ACTA's Report Demonizing Dissent–Part 3 of 6, Los Angeles Independent Media Center. Available http://la.indymedia.org/display.php3?article_id= 13126.

19  Lani Silver, "A Message to Mrs. Cheney: Get a Life!*" San Francisco Examiner,* December 23, 2001.

20  Michelle Chihara, "The Silencing of Dissent: Free Speech is Too Expensive," *Boulder Weekly,* January 3, 2002.

21  Martin J. Sherwin, "Tattletales for an Open Society," Advertisement, *The Nation,* January 21, 2002. Available www.thenation.com/doc.mhtml?i= special&s=sherwin20020109.

22  Jennifer K. Ruark, "Scholars' Statement Says Fight Against Terrorism is Consistent With Idea of 'Just War'," *The Chronicle of Higher Education,* February 12, 2002. Available http://chronicle.clm/daily/2002/02/2002021n.htm. The Web site contains the full statement.

23  Alterman.

24  Quoted in Chihara.

25  Gonzales.

26  Michael Krauss, "Is it 'Blacklisting' or Mere Criticism?" *National Journal,* January 19, 2002.

27  Ayn Rand Institute, "America's Intellectuals: Our Most Dangerous Enemy" (Press Release), September 21, 2001.

28  Paul Rosenberg, "Attacking the Academy in the Name of Saving It," L.A. Independent Media Collective. Available http://la.indymedia.org/specials/ weaklink2.html.

30  Rosenberg.

31  Chihara.

32  National Association of Scholars, "NAS Releases Statement on September 11 and Academic Freedom" (Press Release). February 6, 2002. Available www.nas.org/print/pressreleases/hqnas/releas_06feb02.htm.

# 7

# Schooling America
## Lessons on Islam and Geography

> This crusade, this war on terrorism, is going to take a while.
> President George W. Bush, September 16, 2001

After the attack on America, made in the name of Islam, the media sought to inform an audience admittedly unacquainted with both the religion and a region that is home to more than a billion Muslims. A month after the attacks, Peter Jennings cited an ABC poll indicating that 65% of those surveyed were unfamiliar with Islam; 66% were "worried about a broader war with Islam."[1] Perhaps this latter fact inspired the media to take a pedagogical approach to geography and religion. These instructional moments are the focus of this chapter.

## NEW TERRAIN

The geography Americans learned post-9/11 was of a particular sort. This was not a benign travelogue of cultural and historical highpoints. Rather, instruction focused on the military, political, and economic self-interest of the United States as it became involved in a region in which several of the countries were presented as dangerous and incompetent. And the metaphors used to describe this area were often military.

In an October 11 documentary, "Minefield: The United States and the Muslim World," Peter Jennings unveiled an enormous map, covering the floor and walls of his television studio—a map he strode across as he explained the regional geography. Jennings, the U.S. newscaster, literally walked through the "Muslim world," physically dominating it as he spoke; he appeared rather like Gulliver in Lilliput: "I'm standing in Afghanistan, which for now is very much the focus of attention for so many of us ... and as we walk from east to west [which he literally did], there are Muslims in virtually every country."

One by one, nations with significant Muslim populations were introduced in terms of the U.S. and its popular knowledge; note, all quotes are by Jennings unless otherwise indicated:

Afghanistan we all know.

The Irani revolution was, as you'll remember, inspired by Ayatollah Khomeini, but it ultimately involved the whole nation.

In the last month, you've probably heard a great deal about the Bush administration's attempt to put together an international coalition against terrorism. There are huge challenges and there are clearly some opportunities.

This approach makes perfect sense. A good pedagogue relates new information to old. But the new information was occasioned solely by strategic and military imperatives. In the Jennings quote below, "the map tells the story." We'll see that the story is one of proximity and "infection."

There is simply no more important country at the moment than Pakistan, and the map tells the story. Pakistan right next door to Afghanistan. And a long-time supporter of the Taliban.

China, over here, has a Muslim population about which it worries.

The Chinese share a short border with northeast Afghanistan and have their own Muslim problem. China doesn't want its Muslims further infected by the Taliban's extremism.

Muslims were, then, "a problem," something about which to "worry." There was another unfortunate locution here: China has "its Muslims"— suggesting a kind of colonialist ownership.

The biggest Muslim problem, of course, was Osama bin Laden, whose location was heavily dependent on geography:

> For Osama bin Laden Afghanistan may have been the only place left to go. The roughness of the terrain and the weakness of the government made it a place where he could operate freely.

By and large, Islam was portrayed as dangerous:

> Egypt's recent history proves once again that Islam and politics can be a **dangerous** mix.

> The new wave of young Pakistani soldiers has been encouraged to believe a **more militant** version of Islam.

> [Egyptian student:] This thing with politics is **dangerous**. You go to a mosque, however, and there you find a community and are able to discuss things. A lot of these **bottled up** ideas and **frustrations** are given a breathing space in- in mosques.

> The Islamists turned their attention against **Western targets** because it's very easy to mobilize and to recruit true soldiers against American interests.

> Afghanistan has been beset by war for much of the last century. It was sometimes known as the **graveyard of empires**.

But if Islam was dangerous for the U.S., the risks were painted as mutual. Extending the minefield metaphor, the Islamic minefield became a complex response to American (cultural) "invaders." The commentary below, by an Al-Jazeera correspondent, captured the complexity of reaction:

> On the whole I think [U.S. television] has brought people closer to the Western culture. It has—it has inevitably led to the—to the Western culture invading their lives in many ways and them happily embracing it.

Positive reactions to invasion were underscored. In "Minefield's" introduction to geography and culture, some energy went toward dispelling fears that "they hate all Americans."

> There has been so much talk about fundamentalism in the last few weeks you might actually get the idea that the whole region is somehow mired in the past and that they all hate Americans. Well here's a picture of the Muslim world you probably haven't seen yet. [Clips from Arabic television include "Mad About You" and an Arabic "Who Wants to be a Millionaire?"]

But there was also frank admission that any affection for the U.S. is tempered by dissatisfaction:

> Come up here to Jordan, Syria and Lebanon, you find any number of people who have tremendous affection for the United States, and admiration, too. Who, in many cases, if they can, send their children to come and be educated in the United States. They as Muslims wish to participate in everything the 21st century has to offer. But they also have one other thing very much in common. That is deep antipathy towards the United States for what they regard as its support of Israel in Israel's conflict with the Palestinians.

Notwithstanding this attention to attitudes, most of the coverage in the Jennings show dealt explicitly with the strategic interests of the United States:

> These are all states the United States is going to have to understand better, individually and collectively, if it's going to win the war against terrorism

> For several hundred years, Afghanistan has been a strategic battleground for foreign powers.

> The United States saw its problems in the region compounded a decade ago in the war against Saddam Hussein to liberate Kuwait and, incidentally, to protect the oil fields of Saudi Arabia.

[Saudi Arabia] has become fabulously rich in less than half a century, thanks to the discovery of oil. … The U.S./Saudi relationship is clearly based on mutual self-interest.

The strategic interests noted, however mutual, were not altogether balanced. Two interesting threads to the "Minefield" discussion were hierarchical. The first was its tendency to position the United States as "managing" the region. The second was a definite tinge of superiority. Assumptions of management and prerogative can be seen in the next three excerpts:

You don't have to go very far from the immediacy of the Palestinian–Israeli conflict to another enormous **problem** for the United States, which the **Bush administration now has to manage**. It's only about a footprint away on this map, a day's hard drive say from Jerusalem to Saudi Arabia. Herein lies 25 percent of the world's oil.

So perhaps our greatest contribution could be to **keep other regional players out**, to **keep them from exercising too heavy a hand** … Afghanistan fundamentalists, perhaps, but not extremists or terrorists, where people do have some self-determination.

There are huge challenges, but there are clearly some **opportunities**.

Along with this sense of management came a sense of superiority. In the examples below, Saudi Arabia was a "cauldron of contradiction" and Pakistan was "incompetent."

But Saudi Arabia is a cauldron of contradictions. Saudis practice one of the most austere and conservative forms of Islam. But it is also a country that has become fabulously rich in less than half a century, thanks to the discovery of oil. … The U.S./Saudi relationship is clearly based on mutual self-interest. But here is a problem, Saudi Arabia is a virtual dictatorship. …

[Pakistani author and journalist:] There is enormous disillusion here largely because the elite here have come into power—elected into power and then ripped off the state. Enormous corruption, enormous incompetence, enormous economic decline.

[Pakistan] is a country where many of the schools are run by Islamic fundamentalists, where the most respected institution is the military, increasingly filled with extremists and where the current president got his job after the last prime minister tried to have him killed.

These observations may contain accuracies, but taken together, they certainly did not build a narrative of appreciative or sympathetic learning. Rather, they positioned the "Muslim world" as threatening and full of contradictions and incompetence—this at the very moment where the United States would be trying to build coalitions. A final excerpt from this program makes the point:

[Pakistani:] The public education system in Pakistan has collapsed and so the madrassas, the religious seminaries funded by Saudi Arabia, primarily, are taking up that slack. They're producing a breed of students who have no training or no skills in anything that is required in a modern society. They learn the Quran, they learn the Shariat, they learn things that are appropriate to the 11th century, but not what's needed for the 20th.

Lest it seem that Peter Jennings or ABC were unique in an approach that underscored strategic interest and supremacy, a brief example from CNN's Joie Chen will suggest a genre. In her case, she stood above a three-dimensional diorama of Afghanistan with a pointer, physically dominating the landscape. She assured the audience that Mazer-e-Sharif is "considered key on a strategic level."[2] General David Grange, CNN military analyst, reports:

The area is very important strategically obviously, as you outlined. It was important to Alexander the Great thousands of years ago, it was important to Russians. And I think it's the same thing right now to the Northern Alliance and the international coalition to solve this campaign. It's a key piece of terrain. It ties Uzbekistan to Pakistan through Afghanistan.

As did Jennings, Grange combined geographic and strategic concerns.

One moment provides insight into how different these pedagogies are from those found in the typical international documentary. Joie Chen briefly (seemingly awkwardly) tried to imagine Mazer-e-Sharif, center of the current war effort, as a location for tourists. This was not a rhetorical approach that she was able to sustain, and she quickly returned to its strategic role:

> Apparently one of the most important things about Mazer-e-Sharif is the Blue Mosque in that city. One of the few things you might want to go and look at as a tourist in this city, the Blue Mosque, which apparently is the place where, where Mohammed's son-in-law was entombed, the Caliph Eli was entombed there, so apparently it has significant religious value. But I also wonder, General, if Mazer-e-Sharif, and the fight for it, amounts to something of a real test for the Northern Alliance as to whether it really is allied enough and strong enough to get a hold of one of these cities.

The general ratified Chen's retreat from tourism: "Yeah, that's obviously- that's the big question."

## LEARNING ISLAM

[Female journalist:] My understanding of my world, my understanding of myself and my relationship to God is formatted by Islam.

So began a CNN documentary on Islam, featuring Christiane Amanpour, CNN's senior international correspondent.[3] Post-9/11 articles and documentaries on Islam focused on its peaceful nature. Amanpour asked, "How can a religion of peace have been so distorted?" and assured the audience, "despite the militants' claims, nothing in the Koran, the Islamic holy book, justifies this kind of crime against humanity. … In fact, the Koran forbids suicide." She presented an imam, who condemned the September 11 attacks, "This cannot be a human being. It was not Islam." Amanpour confirmed, "For the vast majority of

Muslims, the terrorist attacks against the United States were an offense against the teachings of Islam."

After providing the public with repeated images of suicide bombers and "jihad," in some sense this was the media's corrective. It was also a corrective to President Bush's use of the term *crusade* to describe the War on Terrorism. The reaction worldwide had been negative. The *Christian Science Monitor*[4] reported that the use of the term "rang alarm bells in Europe. It raised fears that the terrorist attacks could spark a 'clash of civilizations' between Christians and Muslims, sowing fresh winds of hatred and mistrust." Quoting a French political analyst, "'This confusion between politics and religion … risks encouraging a clash of civilizations in a religious sense, which is very dangerous'." Both Amanpour and Jennings appeared to speak for the whole Muslim world when they motivated the need for a re-examination of Islam:

> Jennings: I understand that … there is … a deep desire on behalf of all Muslims that the United States would understand them better.

> Amanpour: Muslims all over the world say that it's time to set the record straight.

And "setting the record straight" involved, first, correcting stereotypes. On CNN, theology scholar Karen Armstrong reported, "The Koran makes it clear that war is always evil, an awesome evil. And killing is always wrong." Amanpour affirmed, "The Koran also teaches tolerance of other religions. … The Koran also says there should be no coercion of religion."

Addressing stereotypes, Amanpour informed viewers:

> The Koran actually has a very positive message for women. The Koran gives women rights of inheritance and divorce that we in the West wouldn't have until the nineteenth century.

And she addressed the issue of jihad:

> To these five pillars of Islam, some Muslims add their own—jihad. But the primary meaning of that word is not holy war, but struggle.

Both the CNN and the "Minefield" documentaries (aired within two days of each other in mid-October) were at pains to note the dangers of extremism, particularly from the madrassas in Pakistan. On CNN, a headmaster said through a translator: "Our aim is to spread the message of the Koran all over the world, and to make Islam prime over all other religions." Like Jennings, Amanpour focused on the education of young children, who gain no skills for the twenty-first century:

> At this school on the outskirts of the capital, Islamabad, about 50 students, some as young as six years old, immerse themselves in the Koran, reciting it over and over until they have it memorized. It's the only thing they study.

She noted that women are not allowed in the madrassa, that "anti-Semitism" is rampant, and that "many of them have become breeding grounds for a political extremism that is framed in religious terms."

But along with the warnings about madrassas, both Jennings and Amanpour acknowledged that the Muslim world harbors resentments for the actions of the United States. Here are some of Jennings' forays into providing voice for Muslim grievances:

> Being that the United States was so closely aligned with the Shah, the anger turned against America after he fell.

> There is an accumulation of resentment about the United States.

> [U.S. diplomat:] It's the impression of indifference to the loss of life by Arabs that has turned many from being warm friends into being, if not enemies, at least skeptics about the United States.

> [ABC news consultant:] How America treats the Muslim world when it comes to human rights is a big issue in the political imagination of Arabs and Muslims. They believe the United States wants dictatorships to remain part of the world because it gives it an easier access to explore the resources of the region and to dominate the area.

CNN's coverage echoed similar sentiments:

Yet the sense that Islam is under siege is quite widespread, even among moderate Muslims who have condemned the recent terrorism.

[Lebanese speaker:] If the U.S. goes on with its foreign policies the way it has been doing during the past 50 years, tomorrow it could be somebody else. There's no finer label to be put on terrorism. I think it's a logical consequence to, most probably now, U.S. policy subsidizing circles of violence around the world.

In their introductions to Islam, both networks left the door open for complaint against America. This is significant considering efforts to minimize dissent at this early stage of the War on Terrorism (see Chapter 6, "'The New McCarthyism'"). But note that much of the negative critique is given voice by newsmakers, rather than newscasters.

There are also specific contexts in which critiques arose. ABC allowed dissenting voices in the context of strategic understanding. CNN aired critiques in the context of what it called "modern-day schisms within Islam," characterized as "The Muslim world's internal struggle" of "mainstream versus militant." In both cases, the amount of dissent presented was quite modest.

The CNN report focused heavily on contradicting stereotypes of Islam. At the end of "An In-Depth Look at Islam," its approach mirrored that of a February *Newsweek* article:[5] They both sought similarities between the Judeo-Christian tradition and Islam.

*Newsweek* began with the differences, the Arab world before Islam:

The Arabs were mostly polytheists, worshiping tribal deities. They had no sacred history linking them to one universal god, like other Middle Eastern peoples. They had no sacred text to live by, like the Bible; no sacred language, as Hebrew is to the Jews and Sanskrit is to Hindus. Above all, they had no prophet sent to them by god, as Jews and Christians could boast.

Muhammad and the words that he recited until his death in 632 provided all this and more.

*Newsweek*'s focus on difference continued:

As sacred texts, however, the Bible and the Qu'ran could not be more different. To read the Qu'ran is like entering a stream. At almost any point one may come upon a command of God, a burst of prayer, a theological pronouncement. … Thus there is no chronological organization—this is God speaking, after all, and his words are timeless.

Whereas Jews and Christians regard the Biblical text as the words of divinely inspired human authors, Muslims regard the Qu'ran, which means "The Recitation," as the eternal words of Allah himself.

But both reports end with similarities. At the end of the CNN program, Christiane Amanpour suggests:

Perhaps for those trying to understand Islam, the key lies not in its differences, but in its similarities to the world's other major religions. Islam, Judaism and Christianity have much in common. All three hold the belief that there is one God. All three can trace their heritage to the Biblical patriarch, Abraham. And all three are founded on the promise of peace.

*Newsweek* ends with a suggestion for religious reconciliation:

[Speaking of moderate interpreters:] It is precisely here that the Bible and the Qu'ran find their real kinship. As divine revelation, each book says much more than what a literal reading can possibility capture. To say that God is one, as both the Qu'ran and the Bible insist, is also to say that God's wisdom is unfathomable. … Here, it would seem, lie the promising seeds of religious reconciliation.

As Americans struggled to understand a post-9/11 world, the media provided them with introductions to a religion, a region, and a culture about which most admittedly had little information. These early instructional attempts invited critique from the left and the right. The imperialistic domination of the map would have been appalling if it hadn't raised a giggle. Aspects of these reports were no doubt parochial, perhaps romanticized. In a speech delivered within days of the *Newsweek* article's release, conservative commentator Norman Podhoretz complained that, in general, broadcasts on Islam were "selectively roseate."[6] These early instructional attempts were, however, noteworthy not only for their content, but because they existed at all. The airing of two documentaries on Islam in a single week–a programming decision all but unthinkable in earlier times–exemplifies the premise of this volume: In post-9/11 America, the public discourse had been transformed.

## NOTES

1   "Minefield: The United States and the Muslim World," narr. Peter Jennings, *ABC News*, October 11, 2001. Transcript available from Burrelle's Information Services.

2   "Mazer-e-Sharif Historically and Strategically Important," narr. Aaron Brown, Joie Chen, David Grange, *CNN International News*, November 1, 2001. Transcript available from eMediaMillWorks, Inc., Transcript # 110113CN.V75.

3   "An In-Depth Look at Islam: The Realities and the Rhetoric," narr. Christiane Amanpour, Mike Boettcher, Brent Sadler, Frank Sesno, *CNN Presents*, October 13, 2001. Transcript available from eMediaMillWorks, Inc., Transcript # 101300CN.V79.

4   Peter Ford, "Europe Cringes at Bush 'Crusade' Against Terrorists," *Christian Science Monitor*, September 19, 2001. Available www.csmonitor.com/2001/0919/p12s2-woeu.html.

5   Kenneth L. Woodward, "The Bible and the Qu'ran: Searching the Holy Books for the Roots of Conflict and Seeds of Reconciliation," *Newsweek*, February 11, 2002.

6   Norman Podhoretz, "America at War: 'The One Thing Mindful'," Francis Boyer Lecture, American Enterprise Institute for Public Policy Research, February 13, 2002. Available www.goacta.org/Norman%20Podhoretz,%202002.htm.

# References

*ACLU Washington Student/Youth Rights.* "Letter to Mark Morris High School" <www.aclu-wa.org/issues/students/PledgeLetter.html>.

Alterman, Eric. "Policing the Academy." *MSNBC* November 29, 2001 <http://lists.village.virginia.edu/lists_archive/sixties-l/3848.html>.

Alvarez, Lizette. "House Passes a War-Bond Bill, but Bush is Not Enthusiastic." *New York Times* 26 Oct. 2001.

"An In-Depth Look at Islam: The Realities and the Rhetoric." Narr. Christiane Amanpour, Mike Boettcher, Brent Sadler, and Frank Sesno. *CNN Presents* 13 Oct. 2001. Transcript. *eMediaMillWorks, Inc.* Transcript # 101300CN.V79.

Anderson, Benedict. *Imagined Communities.* London: Verso, 1983.

Ayn Rand Institute. "America's Intellectuals: Our Most Dangerous Enemy." Press Release. 21 Sept. 2001 <http://la.indymedia.org/specials/weaklink2.html>.

Bassiouni, M. Cherif. "Problems of Media Coverage of Nonstate-Sponsored Terror-Violence Incidents." *Perspectives on Terrorism.* Ed. L.Z. Freedman and Yonah Alexander. Wilmington, DE: Scholarly Resources, 1983.

Baxter, Nathan D. "Welcome, Dean Baxter," *The Chimes of Trinity Cathedral* MMI:4, Omaha, NE, April 2001 <www.brownell.edu/trinity/chimes_2001_04_welcome_dean_baxter.htm>.

Begala, Paul. *Is Our Children Learning: The Case Against President George W. Bush.* New York: Simon & Schuster, 2000.

Bell, Anthony. *The Language of the News Media,* Oxford: Basil Blackwell, 1991.

Berlant, Lauren. *The Anatomy of National Fantasy: Hawthorne, Utopia, and Everyday Life.* Chicago: University of Chicago Press, 1991.

Campbell, Karlyn Kohrs and Kathleen Hall Jamieson. *Deeds Done in Words: Presidential Rhetoric and Genres of Governance.* Chicago: University of Chicago Press, 1990.

Carlson, Margaret. "Patriotic Splurging." *Time* 15 Oct. 2001.

Chihara, Michelle. "The Silencing of Dissent: Free Speech Is Too Expensive for Some." *The Boulder News* 3 Jan. 2002.

Clinton, Chelsea. "Before and After." *Talk* Dec. 2001/Jan. 2002: 100,103, 141-42.

Cogan, Doug and Christopher Storc. "The Ballad of Mike Moran" <www.firemansong.com/The_fireman_song.html>.

Cozens, Claire. "American Ad Body in Call to Arms." *Guardian Unlimited* 2 Oct. 2001.

DeRogatis, Jim. "Stop this benefit!" *Salon.com* 21 Oct. 2001 <www.salon.com>.

Dershowitz, Alan. *Supreme Injustice: How the High Court Hijacked Election 2000.* Oxford: Oxford University Press, 2001.

Eakin, Emily. "An Organization on the Lookout for Patriotic Incorrectness." *New York Times* 24 Nov. 2001.

Eskenazi, Stuart. "Academic Freedom Is Under Attack Since Sept. 11, Some Professors Say." *Seattle Times* 17 Dec. 2001.

Fearnside, W. Ward and William B. Holther. *Fallacy: The Counterfeit of Argument.* Englewood Cliffs, NJ: Prentice-Hall, 1959.

Fenoglia, Gia. "Is It 'Blacklisting' or Mere Criticism?" *National Journal* 19 Jan. 2002.

Ford, Peter, "Europe Cringes at Bush 'Crusade' Against Terrorists." *Christian Science Monitor* 19 Sept. 2001 <www.csmonitor.com/2001/0919/p12s2-woeu.html>.

"Gallup International Poll on Terrorism in the US (Figures)." *Gallup International* 21 Sept. 2001 <www.gallup-international.com/terrorismpoll_figures.htm>.

Gee, James Paul. "Units in the Production of Narrative Discourse." *Discourse Processes* 9 (1986): 391–422.

Geshwiler, Joe. "Panel Faults Restrictions Imposed Since September 11." *Atlanta Journal-Constitution* 4 April 2002.

Gonzales, Roberto J. "Lynne Cheney-Joe Lieberman Groups Puts Out a Black-list." *San Jose Mercury News* 13 Dec. 2001.

Harden, Blaine and Leslie Kaufman. "Mood of Sellers and Buyers, as Well as Purchases, Reflect the Devastating Events." *New York Times* 13 Sept. 2001.

Hart, Roderick P. *Verbal Style and the Presidency: A Computer-Based Analysis.* Orlando: Academic Press, 1984.

Hassell, Greg. "Altruistic Ads Try to Unite Americans." *Houston Chronicle* 25 Sept. 2001.

"Hell on Earth." *People* 24 Sept. 2001.

Hentoff, Nat. "Getting Back Our Rights." *Village Voice* 7 Dec. 2001.

Hertzberg, Hendrik. "Rudy's Rules." *The New Yorker* 20 April 2002 <www.newyorker.com/talk/content/?011008ta_talk_comment>.

"In Defense of Freedom." *IDOF Coalition* <www.indefenseoffreedom.org>.

Jaworski, Adam and Nikolas Coupland. *The Discourse Reader.* London: Routledge, 1999.

Krauss, Michael. "Is it 'Blacklisting' or Mere Criticism?" *National Journal* 19 Jan. 2002.

Labov, William. *Language in the Inner City*. Philadelphia: University of Pennsylvania Press, 1972.

Linde, Charlotte. *Life Stories: The Creation of Coherence*. Oxford: Oxford University Press, 1993.

Lindsay, John V. *The City*. New York: Norton, 1969.

Lipton, Michael A. and Diane Herbst. "Cool Hand." *People* 3 Dec. 2001.

Livingston, Steven. *The Terrorism Spectacle*. Boulder: Westview Press, 1994.

Lowenstein, Roger. "Don't Let Patriotism Dull the Market's Edge." *Wall Street Journal* 19 Sept. 2001.

Lynn, Ken. "The Origin and Meaning of the Pledge of Allegiance" <www.ffrf.org/fttoday/may99/lynn.html>.

Marling, Karal Ann. "Stars and Stripes, American Chamleon." *The Chronicle of Higher Education/The Chronicle Review* 26 Oct. 2001.

"Mazer-e-Sharif Historically and Strategically Important." Narr. Aaron Brown, Joie Chen, and David Grange. *CNN International News* 1 Nov. 2001. Transcript. *eMediaMillWorks, Inc.* Transcript # 110113CN.V75.

McLaughlin, Abraham. "Bush's Two Tasks: Lead, Heal Nation." *Christian Science Monitor* 14 Sept. 2001.

"Message from the President of the Ad Council of America." *Ad Council of America* <www.adcouncil.org/crisis/index.htm>.

Milchen, Jeff. "The Greatest Danger Comes from Within." *Common Dreams Newscenter: Breaking News & Views for the Progressive Community* 17 Nov. 2001 <www.commondreams.org/views01/1117-05.htm>.

"Minefield: The United States and the Muslim World." Narr. Peter Jennings. *ABC News* 11 Oct. 2001. Transcript. *Burrelle's Information Services*.

Morse, Jodie. "Glory in the Glare." *Time* 31 Dec. 2001/7 Jan. 2002.

National Association of Scholars. "NAS Releases Statement on September 11 and Academic Freedom." Press Release. 6 Feb. 2002 <www.nas.org/print/pressreleases/hqnas/releas_06feb02.htm>.

Neustadt, Richard E. *Presidential Power: The Politics of Leadership 1960*. New York: John Wiley, 1980.

"One Year Ago in TIME." *Time* 31 Dec. 2001/7 Jan. 2002: 33.

Pirie, Madsen. *The Book of the Fallacy*. London: Routledge, 1985.

Podhoretz, Norman. "America at War: 'The One Thing Mindful'." Francis Boyer Lecture, American Enterprise Institute for Public Policy Research, Washington, DC 13 Feb. 2002 <www.goacta.org/Norman%20Podhoretz,%202002.htm>.

Polanyi, Livia. *Telling the American Story: A Structural and Cultural Analysis of Conversational Storytelling*. Norwoord, NJ: Ablex, 1985.

Pooley, Eric. "Mayor of the World." *Time* 31 Dec. 2001/7 Jan. 2002.

Price, David. "Academia Under Attack: Sketches for a New Blacklist." *Counterpunch* 21 Nov. 2001.

Reid, Joy M. *The Process of Composition.* Englewood Cliffs, NJ: Prentice-Hall, 1982.

Rodriguez, Richard. "Essayist Richard Rodriguez of the Pacific News Service Revisits New York City." *NewsHour with Jim Lehrer/Online NewsHour.* 14 Dec. 2001 <www.pbs.org/newshour/essays/july-dec01/verticalcity_12-14.thml>.

Romero, Robert D. "ACLU Insists on Need to be Safe and Free." Press Release. *ACLU Freedom Network* <www.aclu.org/news/2002/n020602b.html>.

Rosenberg, Paul H. "Picking Apart ACTA's Report Demonizing Dissent (Part 3)." *Los Angeles Independent Media Center* <http://la.indymedia.org/display.php3?article_id=13126>.

Ruark, Jennifer K. "Scholars' Statement Says Fight against Terrorism is Consistent with Idea of 'Just War'." *The Chronicle of Higher Education* 12 Feb. 2002 <http://chronicle.clm/daily/2002/02/2002021n.htm>.

Rundles, Jeff. "Paying for Patriotism." *Colorado Business* Jan. 2002.

Schegloff, Emanuel A. and Harvey Sacks. "Opening Up Closings." *Semantica* 7 (1973): 289–327.

Scigliano, Eric. "Naming–and Un-Naming–Names." *The Nation* 31 Dec. 2001.

Scollon, Ron. *Mediated Discourse as Social Action: A Study of News Discourse.* London: Longman, 1998.

Silver, Lani. "A Message to Mrs. Cheney: Get a Life!" *San Francisco Examiner* 23 Dec. 2001.

Sherwin, Martin J. "Tattletales for an Open Society." Advertisement. *The Nation* 21 Jan. 2002 <www.thenation.com/doc.mhtml?i=special&s=sherwin20020109>.

Smith, Craig Allen and Kathy B. Smith. *The White House Speaks: Presidential Leadership as Persuasion.* Westport, CT: Praeger, 1994.

"Stellar Effort." *People* 1 Oct. 2001.

Toolan, Michael. *Narrative: A Critical Linguistic Introduction.* London: Routledge, 1988.

"Tower of Strength." *People* 1 Oct. 2001.

Walsh, Joan. "Salt of the Earth." *Salon.com* 23 Oct. 2001 <www.salon.com>.

Wilson, John. *Politically Speaking: The Pragmatic Analysis of Political Language.* Oxford: Basil Blackwell, 1990.

Wodak, Ruth. "The Interaction Between Judge and Defendant." *Handbook of Discourse Analysis.* Ed. Teun van Dijk. Vol. 4. London: Academic Press, 1985: 181–91.

Woodward, Kenneth L. "The Bible and the Qu'ran: Searching the Holy Books for the Roots of Conflict and Seeds of Reconciliation." *Newsweek* 11 Feb. 2002.

Zinn, Howard. "Born Yesterday." *Tikkun* May/June 2002: 32.

## SPEECHES CITED

Ashcroft, John. "Press Briefing by Attorney General John Ashcroft." 11 Sept. 2001, 7:15 p.m. EDT <www.whitehouse.gov/news/releases/2001/09/20010911-10.html>.

Blair, Tony. "Statement in Response to Terrorist Attacks in the United States." 11 Sept. 2001 <www.number-10.gov.uk/news.asp?NewId=2545>.

Bush, George W. "Address to a Joint Session of Congress and the American People." 20 Sept. 2001 <www.whitehouse.gov/news/releases/2001/09/20010920-8.html>.

Bush, George W. "President Bush Salutes Heroes in New York." New York. 14 Sept. 2001 <www.whitehouse.gov/news/releases/2001/09/20010914-9.html>.

Bush, George W. "President Pledges Assistance for New York in Phone Call with Pataki, Giuliani," 13 Sept. 2001. <www.whitehouse.gov/news/releases/2001/09/20010913-4.html>.

Bush, George W. "President's Remarks at National Day of Prayer and Remembrance," The National Cathedral, Washington, DC. 14 Sept. 2001 <www.whitehouse.gov/news/releases/2001/09/20010914-2.html>.

Bush, George W. "Presidential Address to the Nation." 7 Oct. 2001 <www.whitehouse.gov/news/releases/2001/10/20011007-8.html>.

Bush, George W. "Remarks by the President After Two Planes Crash Into World Trade Center." Emma Booker Elementary School. Sarasota, FL. 11 Sept. 2001, 9:30 a.m. EDT <www.whitehouse.gov/news/releases/2001/09/200101.html>.

Bush, George W. "Remarks of the President Upon Arrival at Barksdale Air Force Base." Barksdale Air Force Base, LA. 11 Sept. 2001 <www.whitehouse.gov/news/releases/2001/09/20010911-1.html>.

Bush, George W. "Statement by the President in His Address to the Nation." 11 Sept. 2001, 8:30 p.m. EDT <www.whitehouse.gov/news/releases/2001/09/20010911-16.html>.

Graham, Billy. Sermon. National Day of Prayer and Remembrance. The National Cathedral, Washington, DC. 14 Sept. 2001. <http://user.chollian.net/~b1205/Billy%20Graham.htm>.

Roosevelt, Franklin Delano. "Address by the President of the United States." 7 Dec. 1941 <www.ibiblio.org/pha/77-1-148/77-1-148.html>.

Roosevelt, Franklin Delano. "Address of the President." 9 Dec. 1941 <www.mhric.org/fdr/chat19.html>.

Siddiqi, Muzammil H. "Muslim Prayer of Imam of Islamic Society of North America." National Day of Prayer and Remembrance. The National Cathedral, Washington, DC. 14 Sept. 2001 <http://usinfo.state.gov/topical/pol/terror/01091816.htm>.

# Index

ABC, 43, 149, 154, 157–8
academic freedom, 127, 139, 142, 144, 145, 146
ACLU, 126
Ad Council, 107–10, 112, 116–17, 120–21, 125
advertising, 4, 13, 42, 44–5, 47, 55, 61, 93, 99, 102, 104–5, 107–12, 114, 116–25, 134, 160
Afghanistan, xii–xiii, 14–15, 53, 121, 129, 132, 137, 142, 145, 150–4
Al Qaeda, 14–16
Al-Jazeera, 151
allies, xiii, 2, 5, 9, *see also* coalition
Alterman, Eric, 146–7
Alvarez, Lizette, 126
Amanpour, 155–6, 159
American Council of Trustees and Alumni (ACTA), xv, 127–9, 131–3, 136–42, 144–6
Anderson, Benedict, 6
Arabs, 111, 121, 152, 157–8
Archbishop of Canterbury, 42
Armstrong, Karen, 156
assimilation, 119–20
attack, xi–xv, 1–4, 6–7, 9, 11–15, 52, 62, 71, 73–8, 86, 91, 93–4, 103–4, 107, 124, 127, 132, 134, 136, 140, 144–5, 149

Auden, W.H. 144
Ayn Rand Institute, 143, 147

Barash, David, 127
Barr, Bob, 123
Basco, Sharon, 137
Bassiouni, Cherif, 38
Baxter, Nathan D., 40, 43, 46–8, 58
Beamer, Todd, 98, 124
Begala, Paul, 39, 58
Bell, Alexander Graham, 41
Bell, Anthony, 62
Belnin, Joel, 142
Bennett, Thomas, 99
Berlant, Lauren, 6–7
Berlin, Irving, 122
Berthold, Richard, 128
Bible, 158–9
Bin Laden, Osama, 100, 128–9, 142, 151
Bingham, Mark, 98
blacklisting, 127–8, 143
Blair, Tony, 7, 13
bombing, xii, 14–15, 53, 65, 67–8, 73, 74–5, 79, 87–8, 97, 130
Bradshaw, Sandra, 98
Britain, 7, 13, 41, 42; England, 42, 98, 103–4, 141; Queen of England, 43, 103–4